W9-AFW-170

Matthow

Oriental Cooking
for the
DIABETIC

Dorothy Revell, R.D.

Japan Publications, Inc.

© 1981 by Dorothy Revell

Published by JAPAN PUBLICATIONS, INC., Tokyo

Distributors:
UNITED STATES: *Kodansha International/USA, Ltd., through Harper & Row, Publishers, Inc., 10 East 53rd Street, New York, 10022.* SOUTH AMERICA: *Harper & Row, Publishers, Inc., International Department.* CANADA: *Fitzhenry & Whiteside Ltd., 150 Lesmill Road, Don Mills, Ontario M3B 2T6.* MEXICO AND CENTRAL AMERICA: *HARLA S. A. de C. V., Apartado 30–546, Mexico 4, D. F.* BRITISH ISES: *International Book Distributors Ltd., 66 Wood Lane End, Hemel Hempstead, Herts HPZ 4RG.* EUROPEAN CONTINENT: *Boxerbooks, Inc., Limmatstrasse 111, 8031 Zurich.* AUSTRALIA AND NEW ZEALAND: *Book Wise (Australia) Pty. Ltd., 104–8 Sussex Street, Sydney 2000.* THE FAR EAST AND JAPAN: *Japan Publications Trading Co., Ltd., 1–2–1, Sarugaku-cho, Chiyoda-ku, Tokyo 101.*

First edition: April 1981

LCCC No. 80–84412
ISBN 0–87040–492–X

Printed in U.S.A.

Foreword

Diet is of the utmost importance for the successful management of diabetes. The introduction of the exchange system for the calculation of diabetic diets has made life simpler for patients accustomed to Western foods. The Oriental patient, however, is handicapped as far as his dietary control is concerned. Cooking in the East is done on the basis of a pinch of this and a handful of that. No such scientific system as the exchange exists for the Eastern housewife. The concept of calories, carbohydrates, fats and proteins is utterly foreign to her. Hence, the diabetic patient in the Orient has to forego his delicious native cooking in order to conform to his physician's dietary prescription. Most often, he prefers to continue eating his native food, ignoring his dietary regimen to the detriment of his health.

As a practicing physician, I have been searching for a book which would teach the Oriental patient to eat his native food while allowing him to conform to caloric requirements. Happily, Mrs. Revell has accepted the challenge to address herself to the peculiar problems of Oriental cooking. She has served up a delicious collection of recipes, tempting to the Oriental as well as to the sophisticated Occidental palate. In this book, she has managed to combine the scientific principles of Western diabetic diets with the exotic ingredients of Eastern cooking. She has made life more interesting for the diabetics of both hemispheres.

EE-CHUAN KHOO, M.D.
Thousand Oaks, Calif.

Acknowledgment

A special thank-you to the following: The Canadian Diabetic Association for their permission to use material from their very fine manual, *Diabetes and Chinese Food*.

The Chinese Grocer, San Francisco, for allowing usage of recipes from their magazine *Wok Talk*.

My sister, Marilynn Brant, for editing the manuscript.

The many diabetic patients who showed me the importance of adhering to the diabetic diet.

DOROTHY REVELL, R.D.

Contents

Introduction

"LET THY FOOD BE THY MEDICINE."

Hippocrates, 2,000 years ago

Let's face it. Food is one of life's fundamental necessities, and eating is one of our greatest pleasures. There is no magic about the diabetic diet and no one ideal diet for all patients. Rather than fit the patient to the diet, it is better to fit the diet to the needs of the patient. Situations involving food should be enjoyable. A diabetic diet must be in harmony with the patient's ethic, religious and cultural convictions, as well as with his aversions to certain foods.

Since the treatment of diabetes lasts for the lifetime of the patient, it is important that the diet be individualized. The principles of nutrition for diabetic patients are generally the same as those for non-diabetics. Today, diet principles indicate daily intake in terms of allowed servings from the Exchange List. The list is composed of food groups such as milk, fruits, vegetables, meats, breads, fats and free foods. The Exchange Method is a simple way to follow diet prescriptions. Great variety in daily meals can be achieved by making substitutions using the Exchange Method. Cultural foods and favorite family dishes are easily introduced into the diabetic diet. Exotic dishes, simple dishes, and festive meals can be part of a diabetic diet. There is no reason for diets to be monotonous or unappetizing. Artificial sweeteners need only be used by people who wish to sweeten many things; otherwise, keeping in mind the balanced metabolic needs of the patient, carbohydrates can be used.

Several studies have found that people who eat three or fewer meals a day are more obese, and have higher cholesterol levels and worse glucose tolerance than those who eat the same number of calories divided into more frequent meals. Insulin-taking diabetics should have two snacks in addition to their usual three meals. One snack could be taken in the mid-afternoon and the other in the evening. Basically, the Exchange Method is designed to help simplify diet management. In this method, one food is exchanged for another. The foods listed in the Exchange List are arranged based on the amount of calories, proteins, fat, and carbohydrates in the various foods. Every food included on a given list is equal to every other item on that list; one food may be "exchanged" for another. For example, 1 slice of bread on the Bread Exchange List equals 1/2 cup cooked cereal or 1/2 cup cooked rice or 1 very small potato (see page 20).

From the Fruit Exchange List, 1 small apple could be exchanged for 1 small banana or 1/2 grapefruit or 1/2 cup orange juice (see page 19). The fruit could be fresh, dried or canned without sugar.

The carbohydrates from the Fruit Exchange List are known as "simple" sugars. When these sugars are eaten or drunk, they quickly leave the intestinal tract and enter the blood stream, causing the level of blood sugar to go up rapidly. Carbohydrates on the Bread Exchange List are "complex" sugars. These complex sugars cannot be absorbed directly from the intestinal tract. They must first be changed to "simple" sugars in the intestines. Once the "complex" sugars have been broken down, the "simple" sugars can be absorbed. The level of blood sugar goes up, but more slowly. Carbohydrates are also found in milk. The sugar in a Milk Exchange may produce an even slower rise in blood sugar. This is primarily due to the fact that the fat in milk reduces the rate of absorption of sugar from the intestines.

All vegetables of the non-starchy type are grouped together. These have a high water content and are rich in vitamins and minerals. One exchange is equal to 1/2 cup. The Vegetable Exchange List is extensive; among this group are: asparagus, beets, cucumbers, eggplant, summer squash, and zucchini. Raw vegetables such as Chinese cabbage, lettuce, radishes, watercress, parsley, chicory, endive, escarole and romaine may be used freely in any amount and at any time. Starchy vegetables such as corn, peas, potatoes, pumpkin and lima beans are listed in the Bread Exchange List (see page 22).

Proteins from the Meat Exchange List and fat from the Fat Exchange List are vital to normal health, and while both indirectly influence the level of blood sugar, the immediate effect is not very marked. All the foods in the Meat Exchange List are good sources of protein, and many are also good sources of minerals and vitamins. The Meat Exchange List includes lean meat, medium-fat meat and high-fat meat. All are equal to one meat exchange, but there is a variance in the fat exchange value (refer to the list on page 22).

The Fat Exchange List shows the kind and amount of fat-containing foods used for one fat exchange. One teaspoon of vegetable oil is equal to 1 teaspoon of margarine or 1 teaspoon of lard or 1 teaspoon of butter or 6 small nuts (refer to the list as shown on page 24).

Some items are referred to as Free Foods. Dzerta gelatin, unsweetened gelatin, unsweetened pickles, tea, coffee, decaffeinated coffee and fat-free broth are examples. Seasonings such as paprika, nutmeg, mustard, chili powder and vinegar are found on the list on page 26.

Foods which should not be included in your meal plan unless specifically permitted by your diet are listed on page 26.

Sugar does not bring about diabetes unless it causes obesity first. There no longer appears to be any need to restrict the intake of carbohydrates in the diet. Candies and other sweets are an exception. These "simple" sugars provoke hyperglycemic (high blood sugar) peaks, particularly in insulin-dependent diabetics. As long as the total calories are not increased, the increase in dietary carbohydrates does not appear to cause a substantial increase in insulin requirements nor to induce hyper-triglyceridemia (elevated triglycerides in the blood) during weight reduction. As reported by several researchers, diets generous in starch are very well tolerated by both insulin-dependent and non-insulin-dependent diabetics, provided the levels of calorie consumption are appropriate.

To manage diabetes effectively, you must adhere to the meal plan your physician and nutrition counselor have developed for you, and get adequate exercise every day. Your meal plan is "special" only because the amount of food and the timing of meals has been designed with your specific needs in mind. The foods in your meal plan are not special at all. In fact, they are good foods for the entire family, whether diabetic or not.

The recipes in this book can be conveniently adapted into your meal patterns as the exchange value for one serving is given with each recipe. It is easy to make the substitutions with the Exchange Method. If the sodium content in the diet must be restricted, this can be done by omitting or limiting the salt, soy sauce, and monosodium glutamate content of the recipe according to the allowance given by a physician or nutrition counselor. Avoid the use of salt-cured meats and fish, as well as other salty foods. Although monosodium glutamate has been included as an ingredient in only some of the recipes, it may be used in any of them.

Many recipes in this book are prepared using the Stir-Fry Method. Ingredients are cut into slices, cubes, or shreds, then added one by one to a skillet or wok in the reverse order of the time required to cook them, and stir-fried in a little hot fat. The additions are timed so that all of the ingredients are done at about the same time. These foods are sliced so thinly that all pieces are cooked within a few minutes. Meats should be cut across the grain as this splits the molecular binding. Because of this, meat will be tender and juicy even though the cooking time is less. Red Cooking is a method of stewing beef, lamb, mutton, chicken, duck or carp with soy sauce. The cooking time will vary between 2 to 6 hours.

There are many kinds of vegetable oils which are good for home cooking. Peanut oil is rich in taste and good for deep-frying. Soy bean oil is light in taste, as is safflower oil. Sesame or gingelly oil is used mostly in seasoning and garnishing; it is not good for cooking or frying. The best kind of oil to use should be colorless, odorless and tasteless. Butter or margarine, olive oil or the cream-type vegetable shortenings are not suitable for use in Oriental dishes.

Oriental cooking has become very popular in America. This book can be another tool to help you enjoy Oriental dishes without leaving home.

Bottoms Up, Delicious Foods, Good Health.

Diabetic Diet Prescriptions

These diet prescriptions are calculated to contain 50% carbohydrates, 20% protein and 30% fat. Emphasis has been placed on a reduction of saturated fat and an increase in poly-unsaturated fat.

Number of Portions for Calories

Food Group	1200	1500	1800
Milk	½	½	½
Fruit	3-½	3-½	4
Vegetable A	4	5	6
Vegetable B, used as desired (raw)			
Bread/Starch	6	8	10
Meat/Protein	5	7	8
Fat	2	3	3

As a guideline in following the diet, a daily meal plan, along with Oriental and American style, menu examples, is presented for each of the three calorie level diets. (See pages 13–15.)

The meal plan is merely a suggestion and may be re-arranged to suit your daily needs. If your diet must be modified because of travel, increased or deceased activity, etc., consult your physician or dietitian.

Calorie Meal Pattern

1200 Calorie Diet

Carbohydrates 150 grams; Protein 60 grams; Fat 40 grams

Meals	Food Group	Exchange Quantities	Menu Oriental	American
Break-fast	Fruit	1 serving	orange	orange juice
	Meat/Egg	1 ounce	egg (1)	egg (1)
	Bread/Rice	1 slice (1 serving)	½ cup rice	1 slice toast
	Fat	½ teaspoon	oil for rice	margarine
	Beverage		tea	coffee
	Milk			
Lunch	Meat	2 ounces	beef for soup with	meat patty
	Bread/Rice	2 servings (slices)	1 cup noodles with	sandwich
	Vegetable A	2 servings	vegetables	tomatoes
	Vegetable B	as desired	cabbage	celery
	Fat	½ teaspoon	oil for noodles	salad dressing
	Fruit	½ serving	½ peach	½ apple
	Beverage		tea	coffee
	Milk			
Dineer	Meat	2 ounces	steamed fish	roast beef
	Vegetable A	2 servings	squash/broccoli	carrots/spinach
	Vegetable B	as desired	bak choy	radishes
	Bread/Rice	2 servings	1 cup rice	small potato
				1 slice bread
	Fat	1 teaspoon	oil for vegetables	margarine
	Fruit	1 serving	sliced orange	pear
	Beverage		tea	coffee or tea
	Milk			
Snack	Bread	1 serving	6 saltines	1 slice bread
	Fruit	1 serving	1 apple	½ banana
	Meat			
	Milk	½ cup	used throughout day for tea, soup	½ cup milk

1500 Calorie Diet

Carbohydrates 187 grams; Protein 75 grams; Fat 50 grams

Meals	Food Group	Exchange Quantities	Menu Oriental	American
Break-fast	Fruit	1 serving	orange	orange juice
	Meat/Egg	1 ounce	egg (1)	egg (1)
	Bread/Rice	2 servings (2 slices)	1 cup rice	2 slices toast
	Fat	½ teaspoon	oil for rice	margarine
	Beverage		tea	coffee
	Milk			
Lunch	Meat	2 ounces	beef for soup with	meat patty
	Bread/Rice	2 servings (slices)	1 cup noodles with	sandwich
	Vegetable A	2 servings	vegetables	tomatoes
	Vegetable B	as desired	cabbage	celery
	Fat	½ teaspoon	oil for noodles	salad dressing
	Fruit	½ serving	½ peach	½ apple
	Beverage		tea	coffee
	Milk			
Dinner	Meat	3 ounces	steamed fish	roast beef
	Vegetable A	3 servings	squash/broccoli leaf mustard	carrots/spinach cucumbers
	Vegetable B	as desired	bak choy	radishes
	Bread/Rice	3 servings	1-½ cup rice	medium potato 1 slice bread
	Fat	1 teaspoon	oil for vegetables	margarine
	Fruit	1 serving	sliced orange	pear
	Beverage		tea	coffee or tea
	Milk			
Snack	Bread	1 serving	6 saltines	1 slice bread
	Fruit	1 serving	1 apple	½ banana
	Meat	1 serving (1 oz.)	fish	cheese
	Milk	½ cup	used throughout day for tea, soup	½ cup milk

1800 Calorie Diet

Carbohydrates 225 grams; Protein 90 grams; Fat 60 grams

Meals	Food Group	Exchange Quantities	Menu Oriental	American
Break-fast	Fruit	1 serving	orange	orange juice
	Meat/Egg	1 ounce	egg (1)	egg (1)
	Bread/Rice	2 servings (2 slices)	1 cup rice	2 slices toast
	Fat	1 teaspoon	oil for rice	margarine
	Beverage		tea	coffee
	Milk			
Lunch	Meat	2 ounces	beef for soup with	meat patty
	Bread/Rice	3 servings (slices)	1-½ cups noodles with	sandwich
				6 saltines
	Vegetable A	3 servings	vegetables daikon	tomatoes, celery cucumbers
	Vegetable B	as desired	celery cabbage	lettuce
	Fat	1 teaspoon	oil for noodles	salad dressing
	Fruit	1 serving	1 peach	1 apple
	Beverage		tea	coffee
	Milk			
Dinner	Meat	4 ounces	steamed fish	roast beef
	Vegetable A	3 servings	squash/broccoli leaf mustard	carrots/spinach cucumbers
	Vegetable B	as desired	bak choy	radishes
	Bread/Rice	3 servings	1-½ cups rice	medium potato 1 slice bread
	Fat	1 teaspoon	oil for vegetables	margarine
	Fruit	1 serving	sliced orange	pear
	Beverage		tea	coffee or tea
	Milk			
Snack	Bread	2 servings	12 saltines	2 slices bread
	Fruit	1 serving	1 apple	½ banana
	Meat	1 serving (1 oz.)	fish	cheese
	Milk	½ cup	used throughout day for tea, soup	½ cup milk

Exchange Lists

LIST 1—Milk Exchanges (includes non-fat, low-fat, whole milk)

One Exchange of Milk contains:

        12 grams of carbohydrates
        8 grams of protein
        a trace of fat
        80 calories

This list shows the kinds and amounts of milk or milk products to use for one milk exchange. Those in BOLD FACE PRINT are non-fat. Low-fat and whole milk contain saturated fat.

One Milk Exchange

Non-fat fortified milk

Skim or non-fat milk	**1 cup or 8 ounces**
Powdered (non-fat dry, before adding liquid)	**1/3 cup**
Canned, evaporated skim milk	**1/2 cup**
Buttermilk made from skim milk	**1 cup**
Yogulrt made from skim milk, plain, unflavored	**1 cup**

Low-fat fortified milk

1 % fat fortified milk (omit 1/2 Fat Exchange)	1 cup
2 % fat fortified milk (omit 1 Fat Exchange)	1 cup
Yogurt made from 2 % milk, plain, unflavored (omit 1 Fat Exchange)	1 cup

Whole milk (omit 2 Fat Exchanges)

Whole milk	1 cup
Canned, evaporated whole milk	1/2 cup
Buttermilk made from whole milk	1 cup
Yogurt made from whole milk, plain, unflavored	1 cup
Cream soup, made with non-fat milk	1 cup
Eggnog, unsweetened, made with non-fat milk	1 cup
Tofu (bean curd) 1 block 4-1/2 × 3 × 2-1/2 inches (This would be classified with low-fat milk.)	1/2 block

LIST 2—Vegetable Exchanges

One Exchange of Vegetables contains:

        about 5 grams of carbohydrates
        2 grams of protein
        25 calories

A Grouping
One exchange is 1/2 cup unless indicated otherwise.

Alfalfa sprouts
Artichokes (see starchy
     vegetables on
     Bread Exchange
     List)
Asparagus
Bean sprouts
Beets
Broccoli
Cabbage
Cabbage, celery
Carrots
Cauliflower
Celery
Chayote
Chilis
Cilantro
Chives
Cowpeas, green pods
Cucumbers
Cranberries
Eggplant
Greens: beet, chard, col-
     lard, dandelion,
     mustard (fresh),
     poke, spinach,
     green onion tops
Kohlrabi

Leeks
Marrow
Mushrooms
Okra
Onions
Peas, Chinese pods, 1-1/2
     cups
Peppers, green or red
Rhubarb
Rutabaga
Sauerkraut
Scallions
Shallots
String beans, green or
     yellow
Summer squash
Tomatoes
Tomato juice, 1/2 cup
Tomato sauce
Tomato paste, 3 table-
     spoons
Tomato catsup, 1-1/2
     tablespoons
Turnips
Vegetable juice cocktail, 2/3
     cup
Water chestnuts, 3
Zucchini

B Grouping
The following raw vegetables may be used as desired, any time, any amount.

Chicory
Endive
Escarole
Lettuce
Parsley

Purslane (pigweed)
Radishes
Ramaine
Watercress

The Starchy Type Vegetables are listed on LIST 4—Bread Exchanges.

   Oriental Vegetables and Sauces that may be used as desired or in the amount indicated for One Vegetable Exchange:

Arrowroot, one 2-inch dia-
meter slice
Amaranth
Bamboo shoots, canned, 1/2
cup
Beans, black, fermented, 2
tablespoons
Beans, hyacinth, 1 cup
Beans, winged (Goa), 1 cup
Bean sprouts, mung, can-
ned, drained, 2 ounce
Beefsteak plant
Bittermelon, 1/2 cup
Bak Choy
Bracken, 1/2 cup
Burdock, 1/2 cup
Celery cabbage, salted
Chinese cabbage
Chinese rape
Chrysanthemum coronarium
green
Cibol, young
Coltsfoot
Coriander
Cowpea, 1/2 cup
Fern fonds
Fudanso green
Fuzzy melon, 1/2 cup
Ginger, 1/4 cup
Gourd, shavings, dried, 1/2
cup
Gourd, white flowered, 1/2
cup
Hiroshimana green
Horsetail
Kang kang
Komatsuna green
Konnyaku, 1/2 cup
Kuchai
Kyona green

Labak
Leaf mustard
Leaf pepper, 1/2 cup
Lotus root
Lotus seeds, 1 ounce
Malabar night shade
Melon, white gourd
Mushrooms, black, dried,
1/4 cup
Mustard leaves, 1/2 cup
Nozawana green, 1/2 cup
Osmund
Peas, Chinese pods, 1-1/2
cups or 80 pods
Pickled eggplant in
mustard, 1/2 cup
Pickled radish in bean
paste, 1/2 cup
Pickled radish, 1/2 cup
Pigeon peas, cooked
Radish, strips, dried, 1/2
cup
Seahair, soaked, 1/2 cup
Seahair, laver, soaked, 1/2
cup
Stem of Taro
Stem of Taro, dried, 1/2 cup
Stone leek, 1/2 cup
Suguki green
Tangeh
Taro leaves
Taro root, 1/2 cup
Taro, Tahitian, cooked, 1/2
cup or 10–15 leaves
Trefoil
Udo
Umeboshi, pickled plums, 4
Water shield
Welsh onion, 1/2 cup
Yomena green, 1/2 cup

Sauces

Hoisin or Hoisein, 2 tablespoons
Oyster sauce (see Lean Meat Exchange on page 22)
Soy or Soya Sauce, 3 tablespoons

Vegetables, Salt-Pickled may be used in the amount indicated for One Vegetable Exchange.

Cabbage, green mustard (salt), 1 medium head
        Average serving 1/4 of medium head, free
Cabbage, white mustard (bran and salt), 1 medium or 2 small cabbages
        Average serving, 1 cabbage, free
Cabbage, white, mustard (salt), 1 medium or 2 small cabbages
        Average serving, 1 cabbage, free
Daikon, Japanese radish (bran and salt), 11 or 15 slices (1/4″ × 1-3/4″
        thick)
        5 slices, free
Daikon (salt), 11 to 15 slices (1/4″ × 1-3/4″ thick)
        5 slices, free
Eggplant (bran and salt), 1 medium 9″ × 1″
        8 slices (1/4″ thick), free
Eggplant (salt), 1 medium 9″ × 1″
        8 slices (1/4″ thick), free
Kimchee, salt-pickled celery cabbage with condiments, 2/3 cup
        1/2 cup, free
Turnip greens (salt), 6 small plants

LIST 3—Fruit Exchanges

Each portion equals One Fruit Exchange and contains approximately:
        10 grams of carbohydrates
        40 calories

Apple (2-inch diameter), 1
Apple juice, 1/2 cup
Applesauce (unsweetened),
  1/2 cup
Apricots (fresh), 2 medium
Apricots (dried), 4 halves
Apricots (salted), 4 halves
Apricot juice, 1/3 cup
Avocado, see Fat Exchange
Banana, 1/2 large or 1 small
Berries
  Blackberries, 1/2 cup
  Blueberries, 1/2 cup
  Raspberries, 1/2 cup
  Strawberries, 3/4 cup
Carambola juice, 1/2 cup

Cherries (sweet), 10 large
Cider, 1/3 cup
Dates, 2
Dates, red, 4
Figs, fresh or dried, 1 large
Fruit cocktail, 1/2 cup
Grapefruit, 1/2
Grapefruit juice, 1/2 cup
Grapes, 12 large
Grapes (Thompson seed-
  less), 40
Guava, fresh, 2/3 medium
Guava juice, 3/4 cup
Kiwi, 1
Kumquats, 4 medium
Lemon juice, 1/2 cup

Lime juice, 1/2 cup
Litchee, 6
Mango, 1/2 small
Melon
   Cantaloupe, 1/4 of 5"
     diameter
   Honey dew, 1/8 small
   Watermelon, 3/4 cup
Mountain Apple, 2 medium
Nectarine, 1 medium
Orange, 1 small
Orange juice, 1/2 cup
Papaya, 1/3 medium
Peach, 1 medium
Pear, 1 small
Persimmon, 1/2 medium
Persimmon, Maui, 3/8
   medium

Pineapple, 1/2 cup
Pineapple juice, 1/3 cup
Pineapple rings, 1 large
Plum, Java, 18 medium
Plums (2" diameter), 2
   medium
Poha, 2/3 cup
Pomegranate, 1 small
Prunes, fresh or dried, 2
   medium
Prune juice, 1/4 cup
Rambutaus, 4
Raisins, 2 tablespoons
Soursop, puree, 1/4 cup
Surinam, cherries, 22
Tangerine, 1 large or 2
   small

LIST 4—Bread Exchange (Starch, Carbohydrate)

Each portion equals One Bread Exchange. One Bread Exchange contains approximately:

        15 grams of carbohydrates
        2 grams of protein
        68 calories

Breads

Bagel, 1/2 small
Banana bread, 1 slice
   3-1/2 × 3-1/2 × 3/8")
Biscuit (2" diameter), 1
   (omit 1 Fat Exchange)
Bread (white, wheat, rye,
   raisin, sour dough), 1
   slice
Bread crumbs, dried, 3
   tablespoons
Breadsticks (9" long), 4
Bread stuffing, 1/4 cup
Buns, hamburger, 1/2
Buns, hot dog, 2/3
Cornbread (1-1/2" square)
Corn stick (5" long), 1
Cracked wheat (bulgur), 2

   tablespoons uncooked
Croutons, 1/2 cup
English muffin, 1/2
Melba toast, 6 slices
Muffins (unsweetened 2"
   diameter), 1
Matzo bread (6" diameter), 1
Pancakes (3" diameter), 2
Popovers, 1
Rolls (2" diameter), 1
Rusks, 2
Spoonbread, 1 serving
Tortillas (corn), 1
Tortillas (flour), 1
Waffles (4" diameter), 1
Zwieback, 3

Cereals

All Bran, 1/3 cup
Bran flakes, 1/2 cup
Cheerios, 1 cup
Concentrate, 1/4 cup plus 1
  Meat Exchange
Cornflakes, 2/3 cup
Corn meal, cooked, 1/2 cup
Corn meal, dried, 2 table-
  spoons
Cream of wheat, cooked,
  1/2 cup
Grapenuts, 1/4 cup
Grapenut flakes, 1/2 cup
Grits, cooked, 1/2 cup
Kix, 3/4 cup
Krumbles, 1/2 cup
Malt-O-Meal, cooked, 1/2
  cup

Maypo, cooked, 1/2 cup
Matzo meal, cooked, 1/2
  cup
Oatmeal, cooked, 1/2 cup
Puffed rice, 1-1/2 cups
Puffed wheat, 1-1/2 cups
Rice, cooked, 1/2 cup
Rice krispies, 2/3 cup
Shredded wheat, 1 large
  biscuit
Special K, 1-1/4 cups
Steel cut oats, cooked, 1/2
  cup
Wheat chex, 1 cup
Wheat germ, defatted, 1
  ounce or 3 tablespoons
  (omit 1 Fat Exchange)
Wheaties, 2/3 cup

Crackers

Animal, 10
Arrowroot, 3
Cheese tidbits, 3/4 cup
Graham, 2
Oyster, 20 (1/2 cup)
Pretzels, 10 very thin or 1
  large
Saltine, 6

Soda, 4
Ritz, 6
Rye crisp, 3
Rye thins, 10
Tringle thins, 14
Triscuits, 5
Vegetable thins, 12
Wheat thins, 12

Flours

Arrowroot, 2 tablespoons
All-purpose, 2-1/2 table-
  spoons
Bisquick, 3/4 ounce
Bran flour, 5 tablespoons
Buckwheat flour, 3 table-
  spoons
Cake flour, 2-1/2 table-
  spoons
Corn meal, 3 tablespoons
Cornstarch, 2 tablespoons

Matzo meal, 3 tablespoons
Potato flour, 2-1/2 tablespoons
Rye flour (light), 4 tablespoons
Water chestnut starch, 2
  tablespoons
Whole wheat flour, 3 tablespoons
Noodles, macaroni,
  spaghetti, cooked, 1/2 cup

Starchy Type Vegetables

Artichokes, 1/2 cup
Barley, cooked, 1/2 cup
Beans (lima, navy, kidney),
  dry cooked, 1/2 cup
Beans, baked (without pork),
  1/4 cup
Corn on the cob (4″ long), 1
Corn, cooked, drained, 1/3 cup
Hominy, 1/2 cup
Lentils, dried, cooked, 1/2 cup
Parsnips, 2/3 cup
Peas (cooked or frozen),
  1/2 cup
Peas (black-eyed, split),
  dry, cooked, 1/2 cup
Poi, 1/2 cup
Potatoes (sweet and yams),
  1/4 cup

Potatoes, white (baked or
  broiled, 2″ diameter), 1
Potatoes, white (mashed),
  1/2 cup
Potatoes, hash brown, 1/2
  cup
Potatoes, French fries, 8
  (length 2″ to 3-1/2)
Potato chips (2″ diameter),
  15 plus 2 Fat Exchanges
Pumpkin, canned, 1 cup
Rice, cooked, 1/2 cup
Glutinous rice, 1/2 cup
Tomato catsup (com-
  mercial), 3 tablespoons
Jerusalem artichokes, 4
  small (1-1/2″ diameter)
Wild rice, cooked, 1/2 cup

Miscellaneous

Cream puff, shell only, 1 small
Fritos, 3/4 ounce (1/2 cup)
  omit 2 Fat Exchanges
Ginger snaps, 5 small
Lasagna, 1/2 cup

Pizza, 1 piece (3″ × 4″)
Popcorn, popped, 3 cups
  (no fat added)
Sponge cake, plain (1-1/2-
  inch cube)

LIST 5—Meat Exchanges (Protein)

This list includes not only lean meat, but also medium-fat and high-fat meats and other protein-rich foods.

Lean Meat Exchanges

One meat exchange of lean meat is one ounce (cooked) and contains:

        7 grams protein
        3 grams fat
        55 calories

Beef: baby beef (very lean), chipped beef, chuck, flank steak, tenderloin,
  plate ribs, plate skirt steak, round (bottom, top), all cuts rump,
  spare ribs, tripe, 1 ounce
Lamb: leg, rib, sirloin (roast and chops), shank, shoulder, 1 ounce
Pork: leg (whole rump, center shank), ham smoked shoulder (center
  slices), 1 ounce

Veal: leg, loin, rib, shank, shoulder, cutlets, 1 ounce

Poultry: meat without skin of chicken, turkey, Cornish hen, Guinea hen, pheasant, 1 ounce

Fish: any fresh or frozen, 1 ounce

    canned salmon, tuna, mackerel, crab, lobster, 1/4 cup

    clams, oysters, scallops, shrimp, 5 or 1 ounce

    sardines (drained), 3

Cheeses containing less than 5% butterfat, 1 ounce

Cottage cheese, dry and 2% butterfat, 1/4 cup

Dried beans and peas (omit 1 Bread Exchange), 1/2 cup

Oyster sauce, 6 tablespoons

Medium-Fat Meat Exchanges

One Meat Exchange of medium-fat meat is 1 ounce (cooked). For each medium-fat meat omit 1/2 Fat Exchange.

Beef: ground (15% fat), corned beef (canned), rib eye, round (ground commercial), 1 ounce

Pork: loin (all cuts tenderloin), shoulder arm (picnic), shoulder blade, Boston butt, Canadian bacon, boiled ham, 1 ounce

Liver: heart, kidney and sweetbreads (these are high in cholesterol), 1 ounce

Cottage cheese, creamed, 1/4 cup

Cheese: Mozzarella, Ricotta, Farmer's cheese, Neufchatel, Parmesan, 3 tablespoons

Egg (high in cholesterol), 1

Peanut butter (omit 2 additional Fat Exchanges), 2 tablespoons

High-Fat Meat Exchanges

One High-Fat Meat Exchange is 1 ounce (cooked). For each high-fat meat omit 1 Fat Exchange.

Beef: brisket, corned beef (brisket), ground beef (more than 20% fat), hamburger (commercial), chuck (ground commercial), roasts (rib), steaks (club and rib) 1, ounce

Lamb: breast, 1 ounce

Pork: spare ribs, loin (back ribs), pork (ground), country style ham, deviled ham, 1 ounce

Veal: breast, 1 ounce

Poultry: capon, duck (domestic), goose, 1 ounce

Cheese: cheddar type, 1 ounce

Cold cuts (4-1/2" × 1/8"), 1 slice

Frankfurters, 1 small

LIST 6—Fat Exchanges

One Fat Exchange contains:
> 5 grams fat
> 45 calories

This list shows the kinds and amounts of Fat-Containing Foods to use for one Fat Exchange. To plan a diet low in Saturated Fat select only those exchanges which appear in following list. They are Poly-Unsaturated.

Poly-Unsaturated Fat
> Margarine, soft, tub or stick*, 1 teaspoon
> Avocado (4″ in diameter)**, 1/8
> Oil: corn, cottonseed, safflower, sesame, soy, sunflower, 1 teaspoon
> Oil: olive**, 1 teaspoon
> Oil: peanut**, 1 teaspoon
> Olives**, 5 small
> Almonds**, 10 whole
> Pecans**, 4 halves
> Peanuts**
>> Spanish, 20 whole
>> Virginia, 10 whole
> Pine nuts, 1/3 ounce
> Pumpkin seeds, 1/2 ounce
> Sesame seeds, 2 teaspoons
> Sunflower seeds, 1-1/2 teaspoons
> Walnuts, 6 small
> Nuts, others**, 6 small

Poly-unsaturated fats have been associated with a decrease in blood cholesterol. You may have been advised by your physician to substitute foods containing this kind of fat whenever possible.

*Saturated Fats***
> Margarine, regular stick, 1 teaspoon
> Butter, 1 teaspoon
> Bacon fat, 1 teaspoon
> Bacon, crisp, 1 slice
> Coconut, fresh (1 × 1 × 3/8 inch), 1 piece
> Coconut, shredded (omit 1 Fruit Exchange), 2 tablespoons

---

* Made with corn, cottonseed, safflower, soy or sunflower oil only.
** Fat content is primarily mono-unsaturated.
*** Saturated fats have been associated with an increase in heart disease. Your physician may advise a reduction of foods high in this kind of fat.

Cream, light, 2 tablespoons
Cream, heavy, 1 tablespoon
Cream, sour, 2 tablespoons
Cream cheese, 1 tablespoon
French dressing*, 1 tablespoon
Italian dressing*, 1 tablespoon
Russian dressing*, 1 tablespoon
Lard, 1 teaspoon
Mayonnaise*, 1 teaspoon
Salad dressing, mayonnaise type*, 2 teaspoons
Salt pork, 3/4-inch cube

Miscellaneous Items of Exchange Value

Food	Amount	Exchange
Aburage (fried soybean curd)	2 triangles (4″ × 3″)	1 fat meat and 1 fat
Arrow head bulb	3	1 bread
Bagoong	⅓ cup	1 lean meat
Beans, mung, raw	2 tablespoons	1 non-fat milk
Beans, soy, dried	½ cup	1 lean meat
Bonita, dried	¾ cup	1 lean meat
Chestnuts	3 medium size	1 bread
Chinese sausages	1 ounce	1 medium-fat meat
Dasheen (Japanese white taro)	¾ cup	1 bread
Daikon (Japanese white radish)	1 cup	1 vegetable
Dried curd sheet (bean)	1 ounce	1 medium-fat meat
Glutinous rice flour (*mochiko*)	2 tablespoons	1 bread
Gingko seeds	1-½ ounces	1 bread
Horsebeans	½ cup	1 lean meat
Iriko, chirimen	½ cup	1 lean meat
Kirazu (tofu residue)	½ cup packed	1 lean meat and 1 fruit
Kombu (washed and cooked)	30–50 inches long	1 vegetable
Kamaboko, broiled	6 slices (¼-inch thick)	1 medium-fat meat and 1 bread
Lily bulb	1 small	1 bread
Lotus root	½ cup	1 bread
Miso (fermented rice & soybean)	1 tablespoon	1 vegetable
Mung bean starch sheet	½ cup	1 bread
Mung bean noodles	½ cup	1 bread
Nori, dry (seaweed)	6–7 sheets	1 vegetable
Natto (fermented soybean)	¼ cup	1 lean meat
Octopus	3-½ ounces	1 medium-fat meat
Quail eggs	4	1 medium-fat meat

* If made with corn, cottonseed, safflower, soy or sunflower, oil can be used on the fat modified diet.

Food	Amount	Exchange
Red mung beans, boiled	½ cup	1 bread
Rice, Japanese (cooked)	⅔ cup	2 bread
Sago, cooked	½ cup	1 bread
Salmon roe	¼ cup	1 medium-fat meat
Sashimi, average, many type fish	1 slice (3-½ ounces)	1 lean meat
Sashimi, raw, dark tuna	1 slice (2-½ ounces)	1 lean meat
Sea Urchin paste	2 tablespoons	1 medium-fat meat
Shoyu (soy sauce)	⅓ cup	1 lean meat
Somen or *udon*, cooked, eggless, noodles	½ cup	1 bread
Squid, dried	½ cup	1 lean meat
Sushi, inari with *aburage*	1 cone	2 bread
Sushi, inari with black seaweed	1 piece	1 bread
Tofu curd	3 ounces	1 lean meat
Wakame, after washing	5 tablespoons	1 vegetable
Whale meat	2 ounces	1 medium-fat meat
Wheat fritters	1 ounce	1 bread

Free Foods

Certain foods may be used in unlimited amounts unless you have been instructed otherwise by your physician. The calories are negligible.

Angostura bitters
Clear broth
Consomme and bouillon (fat-free)
Coffee
Cranberries, unsweetened
Extracts
Gelatin, unsweetened
Herbs
Lemon
Mint
Mustard

Pickles, without sugar
Rennet tablets
Saccharin and other non-caloric sweeteners
Soy sauce
Spices
Sugar-free soft drinks
Tea
Vinegar
Vegetables of the raw group

Foods to Avoid

These foods are to be *avoided unless you have been allowed* them in the diet.

Cakes	Honey	Jam	Pies
Candy	Ices	Jello	Sugar
Chewing gum	Ice cream	Jelly	Sugar sweetened beverages
Cookies	Ice milk	Marmalades	Syrup

Recipes

Appetizers

Chicken Wings with Sweet-Pungent Sauce (Makes 27 wings)

> 27 chicken wing drumettes or whole wings
> 2 Tbsp. dry sherry
> 3/4 tsp Five Spices seasoning
> 1/4 tsp. salt
> 1 clove garlic, crushed with side of knife
> 1 quarter-size slice fresh ginger, crushed with side of knife
> Vegetable oil
> 2 eggs, slightly beaten
> 3 Tbsp. cornstarch

1. If using whole wings, cut sections at joints and save tips for soup.
2. In a bowl, combine sherry, seasoning, salt, garlic and ginger. Add chicken and stir to coat. Cover and refrigerator for 1 hour or overnight, stirring occasionally.
3. Pour vegetable oil in skillet or wok to 1-1/2-inch depth and heat to 350° F. on deep-frying thermometer. Drain chicken and discard garlic and ginger. Dip each piece of chicken into beaten egg, then dredge in cornstarch, lightly shaking off excess.
4. Add chicken to hot oil and fry, turning as needed, until crust is crisp and meat is no longer pink. Remove from pan with a slotted spoon, drain on paper toweling. Keep warm in 200°F. oven until all wings are cooked. This dish may be made ahead of time, cooled, covered, chilled and then reheated in 350°F. oven until hot and crisp.
5. Serve with sauce.

> 1 wing equals: 1 lean meat exchange,
> 1 fat exchange
> 100 calories

Sweet and Pungent Sauce (Makes 1–1-½ cups)

3/4 cup water
1/2 cup vinegar
2 Tbsp. catsup
1 Tbsp. soy sauce
1/4 tsp. sesame oil
2 Tbsp. cornstarch
2 Tbsp. water
Artificial sweetener equal to 1/2 cup sugar

1. In a small pan, mix all ingredients except the sweetener. Bring to a boil, stirring constantly until sauce thickens and is clear.
2. Remove from heat and add artificial sweetener.
3. Serve.

This may be used freely. Calorie value is negligible.

Rumaki (Makes 18 pieces)

3/4 lb. chicken livers, washed, drained and cut in half (18 pieces)
1 cup whole water chestnuts, drained (18 pieces)
9 slices bacon, cut in half
1/2 cup soy sauce
1 small clove garlic
1 dried hot red chile, about 1-inch long, crushed
6 thin slices fresh ginger root

1. Fold each piece of liver around a water chestnut, wrap with a half slice of bacon, and fasten with wooden toothpick or bamboo skewer.
2. Mix together the soy sauce, garlic, chile and ginger. Marinate the chicken liver bundles in this sauce for several hours, turning occasionally.
3. Place the bundles on a rack in a shallow pan and broil 7 minutes, turning once. Serve hot.

Note: A hibachi with charcoal to broil or reheat the appetizers may also be used.

2 appetizers equal: 1 lean meat exchange
55 calories

Shrimp Balls (Makes 18 balls)

3/4 lb. raw shrimp
1 2-inch piece green onion, chopped
8 finely chopped water chestnuts

1 Tbsp. sherry
1 tsp. cornstarch
1/2 tsp. grated ginger root
1 egg white
3 Tbsp. vegetable oil

1. Rinse and peel the shrimp, devein.
2. Grind shrimp with the green onion and then combine with water chestnuts, sherry, cornstarch, ginger root and egg white. Form into 18 small balls.
3. Heat oil in skillet or wok over medium-high heat. Add shrimp balls to brown lightly, turning frequently.
4. These can be kept in a warm oven for short while before serving.

> 3 shrimp balls equal: 1 medium-fat meat exchange
> 73 calories

Breads

Basic Bread Dough for Buns and Loaves (Makes 24 buns)

1/4 cup sugar
2 cups warm water
1 envelope active dry yeast
6 cups flour
2 Tbsp. lard or margarine or butter, melted and cooled
2 tsp. double-acting baking powder

1. In a bowl, dissolve the sugar in the warm water. Stir in the dry yeast. Allow the mixture to rest or "proof it" for 15 or 20 minutes until very foamy and full.
2. In a large bowl, stir the yeast mixture into the 6 cups of flour, add the melted shortening and form the dough into a ball.
3. Turn the dough out onto a floured surface and knead for 10 minutes or until smooth and satiny.
4. Form the dough into a ball, put it in an oiled bowl and turn to coat it with the oil. Cover the dough with a tea towel and let rise in a warm place for 3–4 hours or until tripled in bulk.
5. Punch down the dough and turn it out onto the floured surface. Make a well in the center, add the baking powder and knead in thoroughly.
6. The dough may be kept, wrapped airtight and chilled, for 3 days.
7. To steam, arrange the buns about 1-1/2 inches apart on steamer trays lined with parchment paper and let rise, covered with a tea towel for 20 min-

utes. Stack the trays and steam the buns, rotating the trays every 5 minutes, for 20–25 minutes, or until they are puffed and springy. Once steamed, the buns will open up into a type of pocket bread which may be stuffed with any savory stir-fried meat and vegetable mixture.

1 plain bun equals:　1-1/2 bread exchanges
102 calories

Bo-Pe (Makes 12 rolls)

1 package yeast
1-1/2 cups warm water
4 cups flour
1 tsp. salt
2 Tbsp. melted shortening
2 Tbsp. sugar
Meat Filling:
1/2 lb. very lean ground beef
1/4 lb. chopped mushrooms
2 large stalks celery, minced
2 scallions, minced
Salt and pepper to taste

1. Sift the flour, sugar and salt together in a large bowl and hollow out the center.
2. Dissolved the yeast in the warm water and pour into the hollow.
3. Add the melted shortening and mix together well.
4. Knead the dough lightly on a flour board until smooth and elastic. Place the dough in a greased bowl, cover with a sheet of waxed paper and let rise at room temperature for about 3 hours.
5. Oil your hands and the kneading board. Divide the dough into 12 portions. Press out with the hands, then roll with a rolling pin until each piece is about 4 inches in diameter.
6. Drop a good full tablespoon of filling onto each piece of dough, then draw up the edges around the filling and make into a ball. Press the edges together and turn so the seams are underneath. Let rise double.
7. The balls can be baked or fried or steamed on a rack. Bake at 400°F. or steam over boiling water 20 minutes or fry in deep fat at 375°F.

1 roll equals:　1 bread exchange
1/2 lean meat exchange
100 calories

Cheese Puffs (Makes 15 small balls)

4 oz. sharp Cheddar cheese
1/4 cup melted butter or margarine
1/2 tsp. Dijon mustard
Dash Worcestershire sauce
3/4 cup flour, sifted
1/8 tsp. salt
Pinch of white pepper
1 Tbsp. sesame seeds

1.   Grate cheese and mix with melted margarine, mustard and Worcestershire sauce.
2.   Combine flour and seasonings.
3.   Form into 1 ball and refrigerate for half an hour.
4.   Form into small balls and dip each cheese ball into the seeds, then place, seed side up, on a baking sheet.
5.   Bake in 375°F. oven for 10 minutes.

1 puff equals: 1 fat exchange
1/4 bread exchange
62 calories

Chinese Pancakes (Makes 12 pancakes)

1-1/2 cups all-purpose flour
1/4 tsp. salt
1/2 cup boiling water
3 Tbsp. cold water
2 Tbsp. all-purpose flour
Vegetable oil

1.   Stir the flour and salt together.
2.   Pour boiling water slowly into flour, stirring constantly with a fork until well blended. Stir in cold water.
3.   When dough is cool enough to handle, knead in the 2 Tbsp. flour for 8 to 10 minutes or until smooth and elastic.
4.   Shape dough into a ball. Place the dough back in bowl and cover with a damp towel. Let stand for 15–20 minutes.
5.   Turn dough out onto a lightly floured surface. Form into a 12-inch roll. Cut roll into 1-inch pieces.
6.   Flatten each piece of dough with the palm of your hand. To make pancake, roll each piece of dough into a 6-inch circle. Brush the entire surface of the top of each pancake lightly with oil.
7.   Stack two pancakes together greased sides together. In a heavy un-

greased skillet or griddle, cook the pancake stacks over medium heat 20–30 seconds on each side or until bubbles appear on surface of pancake. Quickly remove from pan and gently separate the paired pancakes.

8.   Place all the pancakes on baking sheet or in a baking dish; cover with a dry towel or plastic wrap to keep moist. Repeat with remaining pancakes.

2 pancakes equal: 1-1/2 bread exchanges
102 calories

Sesame Flat Breads (Makes 20 breads)

6 cups flour
1 tsp. salt
3 cups boiling water
1/2 cup peanut oil
1 cup flour
1/4 cup sesame seeds

1.   In a heatproof bowl combine 6 cups flour and 1 tsp. salt and stir in the 3 cups boiling water. Turn the dough out onto a floured surface, knead until smooth, and let rest, covered with a dampened tea towel, for 30 minutes.

2.   Heat a saucepan over high heat until it is very hot. Add 1/2 cup peanut oil and heat until very hot. Stir in 1 cup flour, cook the "roux" over moderately high heat, stirring, for 3 minutes, or until deep golden color and fragrant. Let cool.

3.   Roll the dough into a 14 by 10-inch rectangle on a floured surface and spread the roux over it evenly. Sprinkle 1 Tbsp. flour over the roux and, beginning with the long side, roll up the dough jellyroll fashion.

4.   Flatten the dough slightly and cut it crosswise into 20 pieces, pinching the cut edges of each piece closed. Roll each piece into a 6 by 4-inch rectangle. Fold the top third of the rectangle over the center, and fold the bottom third over the top. Turn the folded dough so that an open side faces you. Roll it into a 6 by 4-inch rectangle, and fold it again in the same manner.

5.   Coat the underside of the dough with 1/4 cup sesame seeds, pressing them into the dough slightly. With an open side facing you, roll the dough seed-side down into a 6 by 3-inch rectangle. Repeat the procedure with the remaining pieces of dough.

6.   Bake the breads seed-side down on ungreased baking sheets in a preheated oven (400° F.) for 5 minutes. Bake the breads seed-side up for 5 minutes more, or until they are golden.

1 bread equals: 2 bread exchanges
1 fat exchange
181 calories

Won Ton Wrappers (Makes 48 wrappers)

2 cups sifted all-purpose flour
1/2 tsp. salt
1 egg, lightly beaten
1/4 cup cold water

1. Sift flour and salt together into a bowl. Make a small well in the center of the flour and pour into it the egg and cold water. With your fingers, gradually combine all the ingredients, mixing and kneading until smooth, stiff dough is formed.
2. Divide the dough in half. On a lightly floured surface, roll out the halves into 1/16-inch-thick sheets about 14 × 14 inches each.
3. If the wrappers are for soup or to be deep-fried, cut the dough into 3-1/2-inch squares with a sharp knife. For steam dumplings use a 3-inch cookie cutter.
4. If the wrappers must rest for any time, cover them with a lightly dampened towel so they do not dry out.

> 4 wrappers equal: 1 bread exchange
>   68 calories

Note: One pound of ready-made wrappers may be substituted.
> 2 wrappers equal: 1 bread exchange
>   68 calories

Won Ton Filling (Makes 24 portions)

1 cup very finely chopped ground or shredded leftover meat
1 Tbsp. finely minced onion
1 Tbsp. vegetable oil
1 egg, beaten
1 Tbsp. finely minced celery
1 Tbsp. chopped scallion greens or chopped parsley
Pinch of Five Spices seasoning
Small piece fresh ginger root, minced
Salt and pepper to taste
Watercress for garnish

1. Sauté minced onion in the vegetable oil. Combine all ingredients and mix thoroughly.
2. Lay out 24 4 by 4-inch noodle squares.
3. Divide filling into 24 portions and place 1 portion on each square.
4. With one finger dipped in water, moisten surface around filling. Gather

dough to form a small pouch and press together so that filling is securely enclosed.

5.   Spread won tons on a kitchen towel or paper toweling and let dry 10 minutes.

6.   In a large pot, 3 qt. lightly salted water bring to a rolling boil. Slip in won tons one by one, cover pot until water returns to a boil, then reduce heat and simmer about 10 minutes.

7.   Remove won tons from water and place in soup bowls. Ladle on won ton soup broth and garnish with sprig of watercress.

> 4 won ton wrappers with filling equal: 1 medium-fat
> meat exchange
> 1 bread exchange
> 143 calories

Soups

Chicken Congee (Makes 5 servings)

> 1/2 cup uncooked rice
> 2 qts. of broth
> 2 tsp. salt
> 7 oz. chicken, raw, boned, skinned, shredded

1.   Simmer rice in broth for 2 hours.

2.   Add shredded chicken and salt and cook for a few minutes until the chicken meat is done. Serve hot.

Note: You can substitute 7 oz. of raw fish for the chicken.

> 1 cup serving equals: 1 bread exchange
> 1 lean meat exchange
> 123 calories

You can also substitute 5 oz. of minced meat, pork or liver or 3 oz. lean pork, plus 1 salted duck's egg plus 1 preserved and limed egg for the chicken in this recipe.

> 1 cup serving equals: 1 bread exchange
> 1 medium-fat meat exchange
> 141 calories

Corn Soup (Makes 4 servings)

> 3/4 cup corn, canned, kernel or cream style
> 1/3 tsp. pepper

2 egg whites, beaten
3 cups clear broth
1/2 tsp. salt
1 Tbsp. cornstarch dissolved in 3 Tbsp. water
2 oz. chicken meat, cooked, skinned, shredded

1.   Boil the broth. Add corn, salt, pepper, chicken and the dissolved cornstarch.
2.   Stir constantly until the soup is slightly thickened. Remove from heat.
3.   Fold in egg whites until well mixed. Serve.

Note: You can substitute 2 oz. chicken with 2 oz. shredded ham or minced lean pork.

> 1 serving equals: 1 vegetable exchange
> 1/2 lean meat exchange
> 50 calories

Dashi or Soup Stock ♯1* (Makes 5 cups)

1 cup flaked *katsuobushi* (dried bonito (fish) fillet, shaved or flaked)
1 square inch *kombu* (seaweed or kelp)
5 cups water
1 tsp. soy sauce (*shoyu*)
1/4 tsp. monosodium glutamate (*aji-no-moto*)
1 tsp. salt

1.   Rinse the seaweed, then place in water and bring to a boil. Boil the seaweed for 1 minute and then remove.
2.   Add the flaked bonito.
3.   Remove the pan from the heat and set aside to allow the broth to steep for a couple of minutes.
4.   Strain the liquid through a clean cloth.
5.   Season the liquid with the soy sauce, monosodium glutamate and salt.
6.   Keep in refrigerator tightly covered until used.

> The exchange value of this is negligible. May be used freely.

---

* Commercially packaged *dashi*, labelled "*Dashi-no-moto* soup stock" may be used freely. To make the tea-bag type, drop one 3/4 oz. bag in 3 cups of boiling water and simmer about 5 minutes. Remove the bag (do not mash it or the broth will be cloudy) and you have *dashi*.

Dashi #2 for Vegetable, Seafood and Poultry Sauces (Makes 3 cups)

> 1/3 cup flaked *katsuobushi* (flesh of the bonito)
> 1/2 inch-square *kombu* (dried kelp), rinsed
> 3 cups water
> 1/2 tsp monosodium glutamate

1. Put the *katsuobushi* and *kombu* in water. Bring to a boil.
2. Remove pan from the heat and set aside to allow the broth to steep for a couple of minutes.
3. Add the monosodium glutamate.
4. Keep in refrigerator tightly covered until used.

> The exchange value of this is negligible. May be used freely.

Egg Flower Soup (Makes 2 servings)

> 2 eggs
> 2 cups chicken broth
> 1 tsp. soy sauce
> Salt to taste

1. Beat eggs with fork until lemon-colored.
2. Bring the broth to a boil and add eggs, stirring constantly.
3. Add soy sauce and salt.

> 1 serving equals: 1 medium meat exchange
> 73 calories

Fuzzy Melon Chicken Soup (Makes 6 servings)

> 2 pieces (each about 1-1/2 inches in diameter) dried tangerine peel
> 1/4 cup cold water
> 8 cups regular-strength chicken broth
> 1 large squab or Cornish game hen or whole chicken breast
> 2 stalks celery with leaves removed
> 2 whole green onions
> 3 medium-sized Chinese fuzzy melons, peeled and halved
> Chopped green onions for garnish

1. Soften tangerine peel in the water for about 20 minutes.
2. Combine peel and water with the chicken broth, poultry, celery, onions and melon in a 3 or 4 qts. pan.
3. Bring to a boil, cover, and simmer about 45 minutes or until the

poultry and melon are tender.

4. Strain broth, discarding bones, skin, celery, onions, and peel.
5. Salt to taste.
6. Serve a piece of melon, some meat, and some broth in each dish.
7. Garnish with the chopped onions.

> 1 serving equals: 1 lean meat exchange
> 1 vegetable exchange
> 80 calories

Lion's Head Soup (Makes 6 servings)

1 lb. ground lean fresh pork
2 green onions, finely chopped
4 thin slices fresh ginger root, finely chopped
2 Tbsp. sherry
2 Tbsp. soy sauce
3 Tbsp. cornstarch dissolved in 2 Tbsp. cold water
2 Tbsp. peanut oil
2 carrots cut in 2-inch long sticks
2 long pieces of celery, cut in 2-inch sticks
5 cups chicken broth
1/4 lb. finely sliced mushrooms
1 bunch spinach, washed and dried
5 green onions, finely chopped

1. Combine pork, chopped onion, ginger root, sherry, soy sauce, and cornstarch mixture and form into 6 balls.
2. Heat oil in a skillet or wok and add the pork balls, turning them to brown on all sides.
3. In a sturdy 2-qts. saucepan, put a layer of carrots and celery. Pour 1 cup of chicken broth over them and set the browned pork balls on top. Cover tightly and steam the balls for 50 minutes. Broth should not boil but just simmer. Add rest of chicken broth, heat to just boiling.
4. Place sliced mushrooms and spinach in serving bowls. Ladle in meatballs and soup. Serve hot.

> 1 serving equals: 2 medium-fat meat exchanges
> 2 vegetable exchanges
> 2 fat exchanges
> 286 calories

Miso Soup with Egg (Makes 4 servings)

4 cups *dashi* broth or regular-strength chicken or beef broth
1/4 cup white miso (fermented soy bean paste)

1/4 tsp. salt
1 egg, beaten
2 tsp. sherry or sweet rice wine
Twist of orange or lemon peel

1. Bring *dashi* or broth mixed with miso and salt to a boil.
2. Gradually add the beaten egg while stirring the soup in the pan.
3. Add the wine or sherry.
4. Place the lemon or orange peel in each bowl before adding the scup.

1 serving equals: 1 vegetable exchange
25 calories

Noodle Soup (Makes 8 servings)

1 lb. thin round noodles
Boiling water
4 cups chicken broth
1 Tbsp. soy sauce
1 whole chicken breast (cooked and skinned), cut meat into thin strips

1. Cook noodles in boiling unsalted water until tender. Rinse in cold water and drain thoroughly.
2. Add noodles to deep serving bowl.
3. Bring the broth flavored with soy sauce to a boil.
4. Pour over noodles.
5. Garnish with chicken strips.

1 serving equals: 1 lean meat exchange
2 bread exchanges
191 calories

Rice Congee (Makes 5 servings)

1/2 cup uncooked rice
2 qts. of broth
2 tsp. of salt

1. Boil the broth.
2. Stir in the rice and simmer over low heat for 2 hours.
3. Add salt and serve.

1 cup serving equals: 1 bread exchange
68 calories

Shrimp Miso (Makes 6 serivngs)

> 1/2 lb. raw shrimp or prawns
> 1/2 lb. tofu, cut into 1/2-inch cubes
> 1 cup strained miso
> 4 cups *dashi* #1
> Ginger root, freshly grated

1. Rinse the shrimp or prawns and parboil 2 minutes in boiling salted water. Drain and remove the shells and black veins.
2. Mince the shrimp and mix with 1 Tbsp. of the miso.
3. Add remaining miso to the *dashi* and bring to a boil.
4. Add the minced shrimp and tofu.
5. Reduce the heat and simmer for 10 minutes or until the shrimp is done.
6. Strain.
7. Divide the shrimp and tofu into 6 individual bowls.
8. Pour the hot soup mixture over the shrimp and tofu.
9. Sprinkle with a little grated ginger.

> 1 serving equals: 2 lean meat exchanges
> 1/2 bread exchange
> 144 calories

Shrimp Soup (Makes 6 servings)

> 6 fresh shrimp
> 6 fresh spinach leaves, about 1-inch wide
> 6 thin slices of fresh mushroom
> 3 cups *dashi* #1
> Salt to taste

1. Shell shrimp and remove veins. Boil in lightly salted water about 5 minutes. Drain thoroughly. Cut shrimp in half lengthwise.
2. Rinse the spinach leaves in salted water. Drain and squeeze out excess water.
3. Boil mushrooms in lightly salted water 3 minutes. Drain thoroughly.
4. Place 1 shrimp, 1 strip of spinach and 1 mushroom slice in each of 6 serving bowls.
5. Pour hot *dashi* over ingredients in bowls.

The Exchange value is negligible for 1 serving.

Tofu and Scallions Soup (Makes 4 servings)

    3 cups chicken broth
    1 Tbsp. cornstarch dissolved in 1 Tbsp. water
    1 tsp. soy sauce
    1/2 lb. tofu, cut into 3/4-inch cubes
    2 scallions, including the green tops, cut into 1-inch lengths
    1/2 tsp. fresh ginger, minced
    Salt and pepper to taste

1. In 1-1/2 qts. pot heat the broth, add cornstarch and soy sauce.
2. Add tofu and simmer for 5 minutes.
3. Add scallions and ginger and cook for 2 minutes.
4. Serve in individual bowls.

                1 serving equals: 1 lean meat exchange
                                    55 calories

Vegetable and Noodle Miso (Makes 6 servings)

    3 cups water
    1/4 cup dried shrimps
    1/2 cup chopped onion
    1 cup shredded turnip
    1/2 lb. very lean diced pork
    1 tsp. salt
    1/4 tsp. pepper
    2 cups cooked *udon* (noodles)
    1/2 cup strained miso (fermented paste made from soybeans, salt and rice malt)

1. Place dried shrimps and water in a large pan; boil for 10 minutes.
2. Add onion, turnip, pork and seasonings. Bring to a boil.
3. Reduce heat and continue to cook for 20 minutes.
4. Add *udon* and strained miso. Cook, but do not boil, for 5 minutes.
5. Serve in individual bowls.

                1 serving equals: 1 lean meat exchange
                                    1 bread exchange
                                    1 vegetable exchange
                                    143 calories

Watercress Soup (Makes 4 servings)

    2 cans (about 14 oz. each) regular strength chicken broth
    1/4 tsp. salt
    3/4 tsp. sugar

2 tsp. soy sauce
2 to 4 paper-thin slices fresh ginger root
1/2 cup water
1 large bunch watercress, stems removed and broken into sprigs
2 Tbsp. finely sliced green onions

1.   In a saucepan, combine the chicken broth, salt, sugar, soy sauce, ginger and water. Simmer for about 15 minutes.
2.   Bring to a full boil and add watercress and green onions.
3.   Cover, reduce heat, and simmer 2 minutes longer.
4.   Serve at once.

May be used freely. The carbohydrate content is too small to be considered.

Won Ton Soup Broth (Makes about 2-½ qts.)

1/2 cup shredded carrots
1/2 cup finely sliced celery, including leaves
2 scallions, thin sliced, including green tops
1 clove garlic, crushed
1-1/2 tsp. salt
Bones and skin of chicken or other poultry
2 chicken bouillon cubes
1 slice fresh ginger root
10 whole peppercorns, bruised or crushed
12 cups water

1.   Place all ingredients except water in a soup pot.
2.   Add 2 cups water, cover, and bring to a rapid boil.
3.   Add remaining water, 2 cups at a time, waiting with each addition until soup returns to a boil.
4.   When all water is added, reduce heat and simmer for at least 40 minutes.
5.   Strain through a fine sieve and discard all ingredients except the broth.

May be used freely.

Vegetables

Stir-Fried Asparagus (Makes 6 servings)

2 Tbsp. vegetable oil
1 Tbsp. sesame oil
3 slices fresh ginger
10 peppercorns
2 unpeeled cloves garlic, mashed
1-1/2 lbs. fresh asparagus
1-1/2 Tbsp. soy sauce
2 Tbsp. sherry
1/2 tsp. salt

1.   Pour oils in skillet. Add the ginger, peppercorns and garlic; put the pan over a low heat. Cover and heat slowly to brown the garlic and ginger.

2.   After removing the tough bottom section of the asparagus, rinse thoroughly under cold water. Cut the stalks and points into long, thin diagonal slices—the longer the better.

3.   Remove the seasonings from the oil with a strainer. Heat the oil until very hot; add the asparagus and turn quickly with a large spoon to coat the slices thoroughly. Cover for 30 seconds.

4.   Pour in the seasoned soy sauce and mix thoroughly. Cover again for 30 seconds. Test with small sharp knife by piercing the center of an asparagus slice. They should be crunchy.

5.   Drain off any excess oil. Spoon into a deep serving dish.

> 1 serving equals: 1 vegetable exchange
> 1 fat exchange
> 70 calories

Bamboo Shoots with Green Soy Dressing (Makes 6 servings)

10 oz. of sliced canned bamboo shoots, drained
1 cup stock (chicken or vegetable) (*dashi #2, page 36*)
2 tsp. sugar
2-1/4 tsp. salt
2 Tbsp. sake
2-inch square dried kelp (*kombu*) washed in cold running water
1/4 lb. fresh spinach leaves stripped from their stems
1/4 cup white miso dressing (page 125)
1/4 tsp. Japanese pepper

1.   In a 1/2 qt. saucepan, combine the stock, sugar, 1/4 tsp. salt, sake and kelp. Bring this to a boil over high heat, stirring constantly, then add

the bamboo shoots. Return to a boil and cook quickly, uncovered, until nearly all the cooking liquid has evaporated. Then cool to room temperature.

2.   Wash spinach leaves thoroughly and pat dry with paper toweling. Chop the leaves with a large sharp knife. In a mixing bowl, using a pestle, grind or pound the leaves to a paste, adding the remaining 2 tsp. of salt. Stir 1 cup of cold water into the spinach paste and transfer to a 1 qt. saucepan. Bring to boil over high heat, then pour the mixture into a sieve set over a mixing bowl and drain. Discard the liquid.

3.   Pour the miso dressing into a bowl. Using the back of a wooden spoon, rub the spinach paste through a sieve into the dressing. Stir the mixture until it turns a soft delicate green. Sprinkle in the pepper, add the bamboo shoots, and stir gently till well mixed.

> 1 serving equals: 1/2 bread exchange
> or
> 2 vegetable exchanges
> 34 calories

Stir-Fried Bean Sprouts (Makes 6 servings)

> **2 lbs. soy bean sprouts**
> **2 Tbsp. vegetable oil**
> **2 Tbsp. sesame oil**
> **10 peppercorns**
> **Salt to taste**
> **Juice of 1 lemon**

1.   Place the sprouts in a colander and rinse under running water. Drain thoroughly.

2.   Pour oil in skillet and add the peppercorns. Heat slowly until the oil is hot and then remove the peppercorns with a strainer or skimmer.

3.   Add sprouts and begin turning them over with large spoons to distribute the oil.

4.   Sprinkle with salt and squeeze in the lemon juice.

5.   Cover and cook for a minute or just until the sprouts begin to wilt but are still crisp.

6.   Spoon the stir-fried sprouts into a deep dish and serve at once.

> 1 serving equals: 1 lean meat exchange
> 1/2 bread exchange
> 1 fat exchange
> 134 calories

Heart of Bok Choy (Makes 4 servings)

    1 bunch of *choy sum* (heart of the *bok choy*)
Sauce:
    2 Tbsp. oyster sauce
    2 Tbsp. light soy sauce
    1 Tbsp. sherry

1. Wash stalks well, leaving yellow flower intact. Lay neatly on plate.
2. Mix the oyster sauce, light soy sauce and sherry. Set aside.
3. Place platter on steaming rack and steam 8 minutes. Remove from steamer.
4. Warm the sauce and pour over the vegetables.

        1 serving equals: 1 vegetable exchange
                            25 calories

Stir-Fry Broccoli (Makes 6 servings)

    2 Tbsp. vegetable oil
    3/4 lb. broccoli, cleaned, trimmed, cut into flowerets, stems sliced
    1-1/2 cups sliced mushrooms
    1 large carrot, cut into 2-inch strips—about 1 cup
    1 clove garlic, minced
    1 tsp. grated lemon rind
    1/2 tsp. salt
    1/2 tsp. dried thyme leaves

1. In a large skillet, heat vegetable oil over medium-high heat. Add broccoli, mushrooms, carrot, garlic, lemon rind, salt and thyme.
2. Stir-fry 5–8 minutes or until vegetables are tender yet crisp.
3. This makes about 3 cups.

      1/2 cup serving equals: 1 vegetable exchange
                               1 fat exchange
                               60 calories

Stir-Fry Broccoli with Cheese (Makes 4 servings)

    1-1/2 lbs. fresh broccoli
    3 Tbsp. vegetable oil
    2 Tbsp. Parmesan cheese

1. Wash and trim broccoli. Cut into small sections, split stalks with knife to insure quick cooking.
2. Add broccoli to hot oil in skillet and stir-fry until barely tender, turn-

ing pieces frequently.

3.   Arrange on serving dish and sprinkle with Parmesan cheese.

1 serving equals: 2 vegetable exchanges
1 fat exchange
95 calories

Steamed Cabbage (Makes 4 servings)

1-1/2 lbs. cabbage
1 onion, fincly chopped
2 cloves garlic, minced
2 Tbsp. vegetable oil
1 Tbsp. sesame seeds, toasted
Salt and pepper to taste

1.   Remove and discard the tough outer leaves and core of the cabbage, then shred finely.

2.   Heat the vegetable oil in skillet or wok over medium heat. Add onion and garlic and cook until pale gold in color. Remove from heat.

3.   Add cabbage, sesame seeds, salt and pepper to the onion and garlic mixture. Stir gently until well mixed.

4.   Place cabbage in dish on steamer rack and steam cook for 10 minutes. Serve hot.

1 serving equals: 1 vegetable exchange
1 fat exchange
70 calories

Uncooked Cauliflower* (Makes 1 serving)

1-1/2 cups cauliflower
1/4 cup yogurt
Salt
Lemon juice
Chives
Parsley

1.   Clean, wash and grate or mince the cauliflower.
2.   Stir the spices and minced herbs into the yogurt.
3.   Add the cauliflower and mix lightly.
4.   Serve on cabbage-lettuce leaves.

---

* Courtesy of: Annemarie Krauel, Dietitian of the Clinic, Center of Internal Medicine University Clinics, Department of Endocrinology, 6 Frankfort/Main 70, West Germany.

> 1 serving equals: 3/4 milk exchange (non-fat)
> 1 vegetable exchange
> 85 calories

Coltsfoot in Sake-Flavored Sauce (Makes 6 servings)

8 oz. canned coltsfoot, cut in half
1 cup broth—*dashi* ♯2
2 Tbsp. sugar
1 tsp. salt
2 Tbsp. sake

1. Combine the coltsfoot, broth, sugar and sake in 1 qt. saucepan, stirring thoroughly, and bring to a boil over high heat.
2. Cook for 5 minutes, then drain the coltsfoot and serve at room temperature.

> 1 serving equals: 1 vegetable exchange
> 25 calories

Eggplant and Green Peppers with Miso Dressing (Makes 4 servings)

1 medium round eggplant, about 1 lb.
3 medium green peppers
3 Tbsp. vegetable oil
3 Tbsp. white miso
3 Tbsp. sherry or *mirin*
Pinch of salt

1. Combine the miso, sherry and salt in small saucepan and place over low heat until warmed. Set aside but keep warm.
2. Cut the eggplant into strips about 1/4-inch thick, 1/2-inch wide and 1-1/2-inches long. Slice the tops off the peppers and remove the cores and seeds. Slice the peppers into rings about 1/8 to 1/4-inch wide.
3. Heat 2 Tbsp. vegetable oil in a large lidded skillet. Add the eggplant strips, turn the heat down to low, and cover. Turn the strips frequently to keep them from browning or burning. Cook until soft throughout then arrange on a serving plate.
4. Add the remaining 1 Tbsp. of vegetable oil to the skillet. Raise heat to medium high and stir-fry the pepper rings. Do not cover. Cook the peppers about 2 minutes until they are crisp, tender and bright green. Arrange the pepper rings on the eggplant strips.
5. Top vegetables with the miso dressing and serve hot.

> 1 serving equals: 3 vegetable exchanges

2 fat exchanges
165 calories

Eggplant in Sesame Sauce (Makes 4 servings)

1 medium eggplant
3 garlic cloves, minced
3 slices ginger
1 Tbsp. vegetable oil
1/4 tsp. salt
2 Tbsp. light soy sauce
1 Tbsp. white vinegar
1 Tbsp. sugar
1 tsp. sesame oil

1.   Wash and cut eggplant into thick wedges and arrange on a deep plate. Do not peel the eggplant.
2.   Set the plate on a rack and steam for 30 minutes.
3.   Prepare the garlic and ginger. Fry in the oil until light brown.
4.   Mix sugar, soy sauce, vinegar and sesame oil in small bowl and stir into the hot garlic mixture until the sugar dissolves.
5.   Place the eggplant on serving dish. Pour mixture over the eggplant.

1 serving equals: 1 vegetable exchange
1 fat exchange
70 calories

Cooked Kelp (Makes 8 servings)

1 large sheet packed dried kelp (*kombu*)
1/4 cup rice vinegar or mild white vinegar
3 Tbsp. sugar
2 Tbsp. soy sauce

1.   Place the sheet of dried kelp in a pan large enough to keep it flat and cover with cold water. Soak for 8–10 hours or overnight at room temperature.
2.   Remove the kelp and cut into 8 pieces.
3.   Pour 2 cups of the soaking water into a 1 qt. saucepan. Add the vinegar and cut-up kelp and bring to a boil. Reduce heat to low, cover, and simmer for 1 hour, or until the kelp is tender.
4.   Stir in the sugar and soy sauce, remove the cover, and simmer for 20 minutes.
5.   Let the kelp sit off the heat for 20 minutes before removing the cover.
6.   Serve.

> 1 serving equals: 1 fruit exchange
> 40 calories

Lima Beans and Vegetables (Makes 4 servings)

> **1/2 cup chopped onion**
> **1 clove garlic, crushed**
> **2 Tbsp. vegetable oil**
> **1 cup chopped tomatoes**
> **1 cup diced zucchini, raw**
> **1/2 tsp. oregano**
> **1 lb. can lima beans**
> **Pinch of salt**

1.   Sauté onion and garlic together in vegetable oil until onion is tender yet crisp.
2.   Add tomatoes, zucchini, and oregano. Cover and let simmer for 2 minutes.
3.   Add beans and simmer until thoroughly heated.

> 1 serving equals: 1/2 bread exchange
> 2 vegetable exchanges
> 1 fat exchange
> 129 calories

Marinated Lotus Root and Carrot (Makes 8 servings)

> **1/2 lb. fresh lotus root**
> **1/2 lb. carrots**
> **2 Tbsp. white vinegar**
> **1 Tbsp. soy sauce**
> **1/4 tsp. salt**
> **1 tsp. sesame oil**
> **Artificial sweetener equal to 4 tsp. sugar**

1.   Peel lotus root and cut in 1/8-inch thick slices, discard ends. Place in cold water to prevent discoloring, but drain before cooking.
2.   Scrape carrots and cut diagonally in 1/8-inch thick slices.
3.   In a pan of boiling water, cook carrots for about 4 minutes and lotus roots for about 3 minutes.
4.   Drain vegetables and place in ice water to cool quickly, then drain again. Place in bowl.
5.   Mix vinegar, soy sauce, salt, sesame oil and artificial sweetener. Pour this mixture over vegetables, cover, and place in refrigerator for 1 hour. Turn vegetables occasionally.

6. When time to serve, arrange vegetables on platter and pour the marinade over them.

1 serving equals: 2 vegetable exchanges
50 calories

Vegetables and Tofu with Dressing (Makes 4 servings)

1/4 cup dried black mushrooms
1 6 oz. block tofu
1 cup konnyaku (gelatinous, rubbery, vegetable root product)
2 small carrots
3/4 cup dashi or soup stock
1 tsp. sugar
2 Tbsp. soy sauce
2 Tbsp. white sesame seeds, toasted
1 Tbsp. sugar
2 Tbsp. white miso

1. Soak the mushrooms in water for 30 minutes or until they are very soft. Remove the tough stems.
2. Cook the tofu in 2 cups boiling water for 5 minutes. Drain thoroughly then place the tofu between paper or cloth toweling to remove moisture.
3. Cut the *konnyaku*, carrots and mushrooms into 1-inch strips.
4. Heat the *dashi* with the 1 tsp. sugar and soy sauce.
5. Add the mushrooms, carrots and *konnyaku* and simmer for 15 minutes.
6. Drain thoroughly.
7. Mix together the sesame seeds, 1 Tbsp. sugar and miso. Add the tofu and mash into small pieces with a wooden spoon.
8. Add the mushroom, carrot and *konnyaku* mixture and mix well.

1 serving equals: 1 lean meat exchange
1 bread exchange
123 calories

Zucchini Strips (Makes 4 servings)

4 small zucchini
3 Tbsp. flour
1/2 tsp. salt
1/8 tsp. pepper
1 egg, slightly beaten
1/2 cup bread or cracker crumbs
2 Tbsp. vegetable oil
1 Tbsp. lemon juice

1. Wash and trim zucchini but do not pare. Cut into 1/2-inch wide strips.
2. Combine flour, salt and pepper.
3. Coat strips of zucchini with flour mixture, dip first in beaten egg then in crumbs.
4. Over medium-high heat stir-fry the strips in the vegetable oil until golden brown.
5. Sprinkle with lemon juice.

1 serving equals: 1/2 bread exchange
1 vegetable exchange
1 fat exchange
104 calories

Rice

Cooked Rice (Makes 3 cups)

1 cup long grain white rice*
1-1/2 cups water

1. Rinse rice with water several times to remove any excess starch. Drain.
2. Cover rice with 1-1/2 cups water and soak for 15 minutes.
3. Boil the rice, uncovered, for 5 minutes.
4. Place cover over rice and reduce heat or simmer and steam for 10 minutes.
5. Remove from heat and allow to set for 10 minutes. Do not uncover.
6. Remove cover, stir with spoon and served.

1/2 cup cooked rice equals: 1 bread exchange
68 calories

Rice with Eggplant (Makes 4 servings)

1 lb. eggplant
2 Tbsp. vegetable oil
1/2 cup finely chopped onion
1 tsp. finely minced garlic
Salt and freshly ground pepper to taste
1/2 cup crushed canned tomatoes
1 bay leaf

---

* If you prefer the medium or short-grain rice, then use an equal amount of rice and water.

1/2 tsp. dried thyme
1/8 tsp. dried hot red pepper flakes
1/2 cup rice
1 cup chicken broth

1.   Trim off the ends of the eggplant. Peel and cut into 1/2-inch thick slices. Stack the slices and cut them into 1/2-inch strips. Cut the strips into 1/2-inch cubes. There should be about 3-1/2 cups. Set aside.

2.   Heat the oil in saucepan or skillet and add onion and garlic. Cook, stirring, until onion is wilted. Add eggplant, salt and pepper. Stir.

3.   Add tomatoes, bay leaf, thyme and pepper flakes. Cook, stirring occasionally, about 3 minutes. Add the rice and broth. Salt to taste. Cover.

4.   Bring to a boil and let simmer 20–25 minutes. Serve.

1 serving equals: 1 bread exchange
1 vegetable exchange
1 fat exchange
163 calories

Rice with Peas (Makes 6 servings)

1/2 cup vegetable oil
1/2 cup sliced green onion, including some of the green tops
1/4 cup minced parsley
1 package (10 oz.) frozen peas
Salted water
4 cups cooked rice
2 tsp. grated lemon peel
2 Tbsp. soy sauce

1.   In skillet or wok heat the oil over medium heat.

2.   Add green onion and parsley and sauté until limp and bright green.

3.   Add peas to boiling salted water and bring back to boiling point. Remove from heat, drain and set aside.

4.   Add rice, lemon peel, soy sauce and peas to skillet. Stir over heat, being careful not to mash the rice grains.

1 serving equals: 2-1/2 bread exchanges
3-1/2 fat exchanges
325 calories

Red Colored Rice (Makes 4 servings)

1/2 lb. glutinous rice (*mochi* rice)
1/3 cup red beans (*azuki*)

1-1/4 cups water
Black sesame seeds

1. Wash rice well and drain off water.
2. Boil beans in water. Two or three minutes after the water comes to a boil, take the pan off burner. Pour running water into pan, wash beans and drain. Add 1-1/2 cups water and put pan on burner. Bring to a boil. Turn heat low and prevent overflow.
3. When red beans are cooked, pour in basket and cover with damp towel to prevent beans from wrinkling.
4. Mix rice with cooked red beans. Pour in about 1-1/2 cups of the water in which red beans were cooked. Place pot on burner. When water boils, add rice mixed with red beans.
5. When rice comes to a boil again, stir quickly and make holes all over by poking rice with chopsticks, so that vapor will come up quickly and cook rice nicely.
6. Set burner to medium heat and let rice simmer about 20 minutes. Turn off burner and let rice stand about 15 minutes.
7. Serve rice with black sesame seeds mixed with table salt.

1 serving equals: 3-1/2 bread exchanges
238 calories

Mixed Rice with Vegetables (Makes 8 servings)

1 dried Japanese mushroom
4 oz. loaf of canned *konnyaku*, sliced thin and shredded
3 cups *dashi* #2 (broth for vegetables)
2 Tbsp. *mirin* (wine)
1-1/2 tsp. salt
1 tsp. Japanese all-purpose soy sauce
3 cups Japanese rice or 3 cups unconverted long-grain white rice, soaked
** 3 hours in water to cover**
1 carrot, scrapped, cut in half lengthwise and shredded fine
1-1/2 oz. ginkgo nuts
3 oz. piece of canned *kamaboko* (fish cake) sliced thin
1/2 cup fresh or frozen peas (thawed thoroughly)

1. Soften mushroom by steaming it for 1 minute. While the mushroom is still hot, cut off and discard the tough stem and shred the cap fine.
2. In a small saucepan, bring to boil 1 cup water. Add shredded *konnyaku* and return water to the boil. Drain *konnyaku* in sieve, run under cold water to cool. Drain again and set aside.
3. In large mixing bowl, combine *dashi*, *mirin*, salt and soy sauce.
4. Using a 2 qts. saucepan, combine rice, *dashi* mixture, mushroom, *kon-*

nyaku, carrot, nuts and fish cake. Stir together gently, and bring to boil over high heat. Reduce heat to low, cover pan, and simmer undisturbed for 5 minutes or until liquid is completely absorbed by the rice.

5.   Stir in the peas, cover and simmer for 2 minutes. Serve.

> 1 serving equals: 4 bread exchanges
> 1 vegetable exchange
> 297 calories

Rice in Vinegar Dressing (Makes 6 cups)

> **1/4 cup rice vinegar or 3 Tbsp. mild white vinegar**
> **3-1/2 Tbsp. sugar**
> **2-1/2 tsp. salt**
> **1-1/2 Tbsp. sweet sake (*mirin*) or 1 Tbsp. pale dry sherry**
> **2 cups Japanese or unconverted white rice, washed thoroughly in cold running water and drained**
> **1 2-inch square of dried kelp (*kombu*) washed under cold running water**

1.   Combine the rice vinegar, sugar, salt and sake in a 1 to 1-1/2 qts. enamel or stainless steel saucepan. Bring to a boil uncovered. Cool to room temperature. This may be stored unrefrigerated in a tightly covered jar for a long time.

2.   Combine 2-1/2 cups of cold water and the rice in a 1-1/2 qts. stainless steel or enameled saucepan. Let the rice soak for 30 minutes.

3.   Add the square of *kombu* and bring to a boil over a high heat. Cover the pan, reduce the heat to moderate, and cook for 10 minutes, or until all the water has been absorbed by the rice. Reduce the heat to low and simmer another 5 minutes.

4.   Let the rice rest off the heat for another 5 minutes before removing the cover and discarding the *kombu*.

5.   Place the hot rice in a large non-metallic platter or tray. Pour the vinegar dressing over the rice and mix thoroughly with a fork.

6.   The rice is ready to use when it has cooled to room temperature.

> 1/2 cup serving equals: 1-1/2 bread exchanges
> 102 calories

Eight Jewel Rice (Makes 4 servings)

> **3 Tbsp. peanut oil**
> **1 oz. chopped onion**
> **2 cups cooked cold rice**
> **5 medium shrimps, shelled and diced**
> **1 oz. diced cooked pork or ham**

1 oz. diced chicken meat
1 oz. shredded crab meat
1 large Chinese mushroom, soaked and sliced
Pinch of salt
1 tsp. soy sauce
3 eggs
1-1/2 Tbsp. cooked green peas

1. Heat the oil over medium heat.
2. Add onions and cook until transparent.
3. Add rice, shrimp, pork, chicken, crab meat and mushrooms and stir for 2 minutes.
4. Add salt and soy sauce and cook for another 4 minutes.
5. Add the beaten eggs, and stir over gentle heat until the eggs are set.
6. Add peas, turn into a heated dish and serve hot.

1 serving equals: 2 lean meat exchanges
1 bread exchange
2 fat exchanges
268 calories

Red Beans and Rice (Makes 8 servings)

1-1/2 cups dried red kidney beans or *azuki* beans
2 tsp. salt
1 cup rice
2 Tbsp. sake
3 Tbsp. toasted sesame seeds

1. Wash beans. Cover with cold water and bring to a boil. Remove from heat and let stand 1 hour. Drain thoroughly.
2. Cover with fresh water. Add 1 tsp. salt and bring to a boil. Cover and cook over low heat about 1 hour or until beans are tender. Drain, saving the water.
3. Wash rice in several changes of water. Place in heavy skillet and add the 1-1/2 cups of water that the beans were cooked in. If it is necessary, add fresh water to make a total of 1-1/2 cups. Add 1 tsp. salt. Bring to boil over high heat; add cooked beans. Cover pan and return to heat to bring to a boil. Reduce the heat and continue cooking over low heat for 20 minutes.
4. Add sake; mix lightly with fork. Cover and cook over low heat for about 5 minutes until dry.
5. Serve in individual bowls with toasted sesame seeds sprinkled on top.

Note: Glutinous rice may be used in place of the regular rice.

1 serving equals: 1/2 lean meat exchange
                    3 bread exchanges
                    232 calories

Noodles

Buckwheat Noodles with Laver (Makes 4 servings)

8 oz. package buckwheat noodles
3 sheets dried laver (seaweed), passed over a flame on one side only and
   coarsely crumbled
2 scallions, including 3–4 inches of the green stem, sliced into rounds
4 tsp. horseradish powder, mixed with a little cold water for a thick paste

1. In a 3 to 4 qts. pot, bring 2 qts. of water to a boil. Add noodles, stirring occasionally, and cook for 7 minutes. Drain noodles in colander and run cold water over them. Drain again and divide noodles into 4 serving bowls.
2. Top noodles with crumbled laver. Garnish each bowl with scallions and horseradish. Serve with dipping sauce.

Dipping Sauce (Makes 1-1/2 cups)

1/4 cup *mirin* or 3 Tbsp. pale dry sherry
1/4 cup Japanese all-purpose soy sauce
1 cup *dashi* #2 broth
2 Tbsp. dried bonito, flaked
Salt to taste

1. Heat *mirin* in 1 qt. saucepan over moderate heat until warm.
2. Turn off heat, ignite *mirin* with a match, and shake pan gently until flame dies out.
3. Add soy sauce, *dashi*, bonito and pinch of salt. Bring to boil over high heat, then strain sauce through a fine sieve set over a small bowl. Cool to room temperature.

1 serving of noodles equals: 2-1/2 bread exchanges
                               1 vegetable exchange
        1/4 cup sauce equals: 1 vegetable exchange
                               220 calories for total

Chilled Somen—Full Moon (Makes 6 servings)

1 pound noodles (*somen*)
2 cups *dashi* #2

4 Tbsp. soy sauce
1 Tbsp. sugar
1 tsp. monosodium glutamate
6 uncooked eggs

1. Cook the noodles in unsalted boiling water until tender.
2. Rinse thoroughly in cold water and drain. Chill.
3. Combine the *dashi*, soy sauce, sugar and monosodium glutamate in saucepan. Heat to boiling.
4. Remove the liquid from the heat and chill.
5. Divide the noodles equally into 6 individual serving bowls.
6. Top each bowl of noodles with 1 uncooked egg.
7. Pour chilled sauce over the egg-noodles dish and serve cold.

> 1 serving equals: 1 medium-meat exchange
> 3 bread exchanges
> 277 calories

Taro Potatoes Rolled in Crumbled Seaweed (Makes 4 servings)

1 tsp. sugar
1 tsp. salt
1-1/2 cups chicken broth or *dashi* #2
8 canned taro potatoes, drained (medium size)
1 sheet dried seaweed (laver, *nori*)

1. Combine the sugar, salt and broth in a 1 qt. saucepan and bring to a boil over high heat.
2. Add the taro potatoes, stir gently, and reduce the heat to low.
3. Simmer, uncovered for 6–8 minutes, then remove from the heat and cool.
4. Pass the sheet of seaweed over flame or electric burner of the stove on one side to intensify the color and flavor.
5. Crumble the seaweed on a sheet of wax paper.
6. Remove the potatoes from the liquid and roll them one at a time in the crumbled seaweed to coat them evenly.
7. Serve.

> 2 potatoes equal: 1 bread exchange
> 68 calories

Custards

Egg Custard (Makes 4 servings)

> 2 cups *dashi* #2 broth
> 6 eggs, beaten
> 1 tsp. Japanese soy sauce
> 2 Tbsp. sake
> Artificial sweetener equal to 1/2 tsp. sugar
> 3/4 tsp. salt
> 2/3 cup *dashi* #2 broth
> 2 Tbsp. Japanese soy sauce
> Vegetable oil

1. Mix the eggs, soup broth, soy sauce, sake, artificial sweetener, and salt.
2. Lightly cover the inside of a square pan (5–7 inches square and 1–2 inches deep) with vegetable oil. Pour in egg mixture.
3. Heat steamer and place pan on rack.
4. Steam for 3 minutes using medium heat then on low heat for 10 minutes. Test with a tooth pick. It should come out clean when stuck into the custard.
5. Cool custard and loosen edges with fingers.
6. Place pan in water and cut into fourths while still in the pan. Scoop out each piece with your hand or spatula. Cut each piece into thirds and allow water to drain.
7. Place pieces on serving places.
8. Add soy sauce to broth and boil. Cool thoroughly. Pour broth over egg custard.

> 1 serving equals: 1-1/2 medium-fat meat exchanges
> 109 calories

Chicken and Fish Custard (Makes 6 servings)

> 1 cup cooked white meat chicken, cut into small pieces
> 2 Tbsp. soy sauce
> 12 large cooked shrimp, peeled and deveined
> 1-1/2 cups spinach, washed with stems removed
> 6 large mushrooms, cut in half
> 6 thin slices of lemon
> 3 cups regular strength chicken broth or *dashi*
> 6 eggs, well beaten
> 1/4 tsp. salt

1. Mix the chicken and soy sauce together.
2. Place equal amounts of chicken, shrimp, spinach, mushrooms and lemon in 6 individual serving bowls or cups.
3. Fill cups with broth beaten with the egg and salt.
4. Place bowls or cups in large shallow pan of hot water over direct heat. Cover the cups with lids or a baking sheet.
5. Poach in hot, not boiling, water until custard is firm in the center. This takes about 30 minutes. Serve hot.

Note: Because of the low fat content of the meat and shrimp 1/2 extra fat exchange may be allowed in the diet.

> 1 serving equals: 3 lean meat exchanges
> 140 calories

Custard with Fish, Meat and Vegetables (Makes 4 servings)

> **4 medium fresh shrimp**
> **4 oz. chicken, cooked, boned and skinned**
> **1/2 tsp. soy sauce**
> **4 eggs**
> **2-1/2 cups *dashi* ♯1 or broth**
> **1/2 tsp. salt**
> **4 small mushrooms**
> **12 snow peas**

1. Shell and devein the shrimp.
2. Dice chicken into 1/2-inch chunks and soak in the soy sauce for a few minutes.
3. Arrange shrimp, chicken, mushrooms and snow peas in equal portions in 4 individual bowls or cups.
4. Beat the eggs, add the *dashi* or broth and salt. Pour the egg mixture into each bowl.
5. Place tops on the bowls or cups, or cover them tightly with aluminum foil.
6. Place the covered bowls on a steamer rack over boiling water. Cover the steamer and cook over medium-low heat for about 30 minutes. Remove the hot bowls from steamer, set on a small plate and serve hot.

> 1 serving equals: 2 lean meat exchanges
> Carbohydrate content is negligible.
> 110 calories

Custard with Noodles, Meat and Vegetables (Makes 4 servings)

1-1/2 cups cooked *udon* or noodles
1 Tbsp. soy sauce
3 eggs
2 cups *dashi* #1 or broth
1 tsp. sherry or *mirin*
1 tsp. soy sauce
Dash of salt
4 small mushrooms, fresh or dried
3/4 cup sliced *kamaboko* (fish cake or white meat of cooked chicken)
4 small sprigs of celery greens, chopped

1.   Sprinkle 1 Tbsp. of soy sauce over the cooked *udon*, toss and let rest for 10 minutes so the soy sauce may be absorbed.
2.   Beat the eggs, add *dashi*, *mirin*, 1 tsp. soy sauce and salt.
3.   If dried mushrooms are used, soak them 30 minutes in water. Cut off and discard the tough stems. Slice mushrooms when they have rehydrated. Fresh mushrooms may be sliced at once.
4.   Place the cooked noodles or *udon* in 4 small bowls. Arrange the *kamaboko* or meat, mushrooms and celery greens over the noodles. Pour the egg mixture over them, then cover with a lid or aluminum foil. Place bowls on steaming rack and steam 20 minutes over medium-low heat.
5.   Remove the hot bowls from steamer and set on small plates. Serve hot.

1 serving equals: 1 medium-fat meat exchange
1 bread exchange
141 calories

Steamed Shrimp-Chicken-Custard (Makes 4 servings)

4 medium size shrimp, raw, peeled, deveined, cut in half lengthwise
1/4 tsp. salt
1/2 chicken breast, boned, skinned, cut into small cubes
1/4 tsp. Japanese all-purpose soy sauce
12 canned ginkgo nuts
Custard:
4 medium-size eggs, beaten thoroughly
2-2/3 cups *dashi* #2 broth
1/2 tsp. salt
1/4 tsp. light soy sauce
Garnish:
Parsley sprigs

1.   Sprinkle the shrimp with salt; sprinkle the chicken with soy sauce.
2.   Equally divide shrimp and chicken into four 8-ounce cups or bowls.

3. In mixing bowl, stir *dashi*, salt, soy sauce and beaten eggs.

4. Equally divide the egg mixture among the 4 cups. Cover each with lid or aluminum foil.

5. Place cups in water bath or steamer and bring the water to a boil, then partially cover the steamer and steam over moderate heat for 10 minutes or until custard is firm.

6. Garnish with parsley sprigs.

1 serving equals: 2 lean meat exchanges
110 calories

Eggs

Egg Foo Yong (Makes 4 servings)

> **4 eggs**
> **1 Tbsp. soy sauce**
> **3/4 cup cooked pork, trimmed of fat, shredded**
> **1 cup bean sprouts, blanched**
> **1/2 cup onion, thinly sliced**
> **1/2 cup celery, thinly sliced, blanched**
> **1/4 cup vegetable oil**

1. Beat eggs with soy sauce.
2. Add shredded pork, bean sprouts and vegetables; stir well.
3. Heat vegetable oil in skillet or wok over medium heat.
4. Spoon 2 Tbsp. of egg mixture at a time into the oil to cook into separate small omelets.
5. Cook about 2 minutes to brown bottom, turn with slotted spatula, brown other side. Lift out, drain on paper toweling.
6. Repeat with remaining mixture. Serve with sauce.

1 serving equals: 2 medium-fat meat exchanges
1 vegetable exchange
2 fat exchanges
261 calories

Sauce

> **1 Tbsp. vegetable oil**
> **2 scallions, thinly sliced**
> **3/4 cup chicken broth**
> **1 Tbsp. catsup**
> **Dash of hot pepper**
> **1 Tbsp. of corn starch dissolved in 2 Tbsp. water**

Heat vegetable oil in small sauce pan and add the other ingredients, stir constantly until mixture is thick and clear.

Sauce may be used freely. Calories are negligible.

Shrimp Foo Yung (Makes 4 servings)

4 oz. shrimp, shelled, deveined
2 cups mung bean sprouts
1 tsp. salt
2 oz. barbecued pork
4 medium size eggs
3 Tbsp. vegetable oil

1.   Over medium heat stir-fry the shrimp in 1/2 Tbsp. of oil for 1 minute. Set aside.
2.   Stir-fry the bean sprouts in 1/2 Tbsp. oil for about 1 minute. Set aside.
3.   Shred the barbecued pork.
4.   Beat the eggs. Add salt, bean sprouts and barbecued pork.
5.   Heat 2 Tbsp. vegetable oil, pan-fry the egg mixture over low heat until the egg mixture is set.
6.   Add the shrimp. Stir-fry to combine. Serve.

Note: You may substitute 4 oz. shrimp and 2 oz. barbecued pork with 6 oz. of one or more kinds of meat (e.g. 6 oz. minced beef, or 3 oz. shredded chicken meat and 3 oz. shredded liver).

1 serving equals: 1 vegetable exchange
2 medium-fat meat exchanges
261 calories

Shrimp Egg Foo Yong (Makes 2 servings)

4 eggs
1/2 cup boiled shrimp, chopped
1 cup canned mushrooms, drained, chopped
2 green onions
1/4 tsp. salt
1/2 tsp. soy sauce
1 Tbsp. vegetable oil

1.   Mix all ingredients in large bowl.
2.   Heat oil in skillet and swirl the oil to coat the bottom and sides.
3.   Pour mixture into the skillet, brown on one side, turn with a spatula to form a roll.

4. Slice in pieces to serve.

1 serving equals: 3 medium-fat meat exchanges
219 calories

Eggs, Shrimps and Vegetables (Makes 4 servings)

4 Tbsp. vegetable oil
1/2 cup sliced celery
1/4 cup green onions, cut in 1/4-inch lengths
3/4 lb. shrimp, sliced
1-1/2 tsp. soy sauce
3/4 tsp. salt
Few grains pepper

1. Beat eggs with fork until lemon-colored.
2. Add 1 Tbsp. oil to skillet, heat and sauté the vegetable for 3 seconds.
3. Remove vegetables.
4. Reheat the skillet, add 1 Tbsp. of oil and sauté the shrimp for 2 minutes. Remove.
5. Add vegetables, shrimp, soy sauce, salt and pepper to eggs and mix well.
6. Heat pan and add 1 Tbsp. of oil. Pour 1/2 of mixture into pan, brown on both sides. Remove to serving plate.
7. Repeat by adding the last half to the heated pan to which has been added 1 Tbsp. oil.

1 serving equals: 4 medium-fat meat exchanges
292 calories

Crab-Meat Egg Pancakes (Makes 4 servings)

1 cup fresh or canned crab meat
1/2 cup celery, finely chopped
2 Tbsp. scallions, minced
Salt and pepper
4 eggs, well beaten
3 Tbsp. vegetable oil

1. Heat 3 Tbsp. oil in heavy skillet.
2. Mix the beaten eggs into the rest of the ingredients and pour into skillet.
3. Cook over a low heat until the pancake is well set.
4. Cut into quarters and turn each section carefully.

5. Avoid overcooking as it will toughen the pancake.

1 quarter serving equals: 2 medium-fat meat exchanges
1 fat exchange
201 calories

Bean Curd

Buddha's Dish—Lo Hon Chai* (Makes 4 servings)

2 blocks of bean curd (4-1/2 × 3 × 2-1/2-inches), cut in halves to serve 4
2 Tbsp. dark Chinese soy sauce
2 Tbsp. light Chinese soy sauce
1/4 tsp. Five-Spice Powder
1/2 tsp. monosodium glutamate (omit if on a sodium restriction)
2 Tbsp. vegetable oil
1/4 cup green onion with 6-inches of stem
1/2 cup soaked black mushrooms
1/2 cup carrots, sliced thin vertically
1/2 bell pepper, thin sliced
1/2 cup chili pepper
1/2 cup bamboo shoots

1. Place bean curd on a towel on cutting board. Place another towel on top. Place a heavy object on top and leave overnight to squeeze out all the moisture.

2. Marinate bean squares in mixture of 1 Tbsp. dark soy sauce, Five Spice Powder, and 1/4 tsp. monosodium glutamate (if used), for 2 hours.

3. Preheat oven to high temperature, put the marinated bean curd on a pan in the oven, then immediately lower the heat to 200°F., baking 2 or 3 hours in order to dry out the bean curd completely.

4. Cool in refrigerator before slicing. When cool, slice each square into 2 squares, then put one on top of the other and slice into strips as thin as you can.

5. Put 2 Tbsp. of vegetable oil in skillet, and quick-fry the green onion and black mushrooms for 1 minute. Add the bean curds for 1 minute, then stir in the carrots and peppers and fry for 1 more minute.

6. Now add bamboo shoots, 1 Tbsp. dark soy sauce, 1 tsp. light soy sauce, and 1/4 tsp. monosodium glutamate (if used). Stir and serve immediately.

---

* Recipe used with the courtesy of: Madame Wu's *Art of Chinese Cooking*, Charles Publishing Company.

1 serving equals: 3 lean meat exchanges
1 vegetable exchange
190 calories

Fried Soya Bean Curd and Egg (Makes 4 servings)

2 blocks soya bean curd, deep-fried and drained
2 eggs
2 oz. bean sprouts
2 cucumbers
Oil for frying
Sauce:
  1 Tbsp. peanut butter
  2 Tbsp. soya sauce
  1 Tbsp. water
  1 clove garlic, grated
  1 tsp. lemon juice

1. Cut the fried bean curd into large squares.
2. Beat the eggs.
3. Dip the bean curd in egg mixture and deep-fry until golden brown. Drain on paper.
3. Peel the cucumber, cut into 1/2-inch squares.
4. Boil the bean sprouts lightly and drain.
5. When time to serve, arrange the above items in a dish. Pour the sauce over.
6. To prepare the sauce: mix the peanut butter and garlic. Add the soy sauce, water and lemon juice. Stir and bring to a boil.

1 serving equals: 3/4 cup whole milk exchange
1/2 lean meat exchange
1 fat exchange
172 calories

Tofu Loaf (Makes 6 servings)

2 lb. tofu curd
1/4 cup chopped onion
1/4 cup chopped celery
2 Tbsp. vegetable oil
1/4 cup mayonnaise
1/4 cup soy sauce
2 tsp. monosodium glutamate (omit on sodium restriction diet)
3/4 cup dry bread crumbs (3 slices of bread)
1/8 tsp. garlic powder
1/8 tsp. sage

1. Drain tofu and mash.
2. Brush loaf pan with oil.
3. Sauté onion and celery in remaining oil.
4. Combine all ingredients and mix well.
5. Bake in loaf pan or form into patties and bake at 375° F. for 40 minutes or until brown.

1 serving equals: 2 lean meat exchanges
1/2 bread exchange
2 fat exchanges
234 calories

Spicy Soybean Curd (Makes 5 servings)

2 oz. pork or beef, minced
4 blocks soybean curd
1 Tbsp. green onion, chopped
1 Tbsp. chili oil
1-1/2 Tbsp. yellow bean sauce
2 tsp. soy sauce
1 tsp. pepper
Dash of salt
1/2 cup water
1 Tbsp. vegetable oil
1/4 tsp. cornstarch
1/8 tsp. sesame oil

1. Cut the soybean curd into 1/2-inch cubes. Place in boiled water for a few minutes, then drain off.
2. Heat the oil in skillet over medium-high heat. Add minced pork, yellow bean sauce, pepper, soy sauce, chili oil, salt and garlic. Stir-fry to mix.
3. Add soy bean curd, water and cornstarch. Cook over low heat for a few minutes.
4. Add chopped green onion and sesame oil. Serve at once.

Note: Sake sauce may be substituted for the chili oil.

1 serving equals: 1 vegetable exchange
2 medium-fat meat exchanges
1 fat exchange
216 calories

Chicken

Fried Chicken (Makes 6 servings)

>   **2-1/2 lb. fryer, cut into pieces**
> **Marinade:**
>   **4 Tbsp. soy sauce**
>   **2 tsp.** *mirin* **or sherry**
>   **Juice of 1 lemon**
>   **Dash of salt**
>   **Dash of paprika**
>   **4 Tbsp. cornstarch**
>   **4 Tbsp. vegetable oil for frying chicken**

1. Wash chicken and pat dry with paper toweling.
2. Mix together the soy sauce, *mirin*, lemon juice, salt and paprika.
3. Marinate chicken pieces in marinade for 2 hours, drain off excess liquid.
4. Sprinkle chicken with cornstarch.
5. Heat oil in skillet or wok over medium heat. Fry chicken until tender and browned, turning over the pieces frequently.
6. Drain each piece of chicken on paper toweling.
7. May be served or kept warm in heated oven.

>   1 serving equals: 3 medium-fat meat exchanges
>   1/2 fat exchange
>   1/2 bread exchange
>   273 calories

Chicken Simmered in Seasoned Broth (Umani) (Makes 4 servings)

>   **1/2 lb. chicken breasts, boned, skinned**
>   **4 medium dried mushrooms or /14 lb. fresh mushrooms**
>   **1** *gobo* **root or 1 medium potato**
>   **2 carrots**
>   **1 block** *konnyaku* **or 1 small zucchini**
>   **1 cup bamboo shoots**
>   **1 medium onion**
>   **1 Tbsp. vegetable oil**
>   **1 cup** *dashi* **#1 or chicken broth**
>   **2 tsp. Japanese all-purpose soy sauce**
>   **1/2 cup fresh or frozen green peas**

1. Soak dried mushrooms in water for 30 minutes or until soft. Cut off and discard tough stems. Slice mushrooms into strips about 1/4-inch wide.

If fresh mushrooms are used, cut these into thirds.

2. Scrape the *gobo* under cool running water and cut into chunks about 1-inch long; soak pieces in bowl of water to remove the bitterness. If potatoes are used, peel and cut into chunks about 3/4-inch cubes.

3. Peel the carrots and slice into circles about 1/2-inch thick. Slice bamboo shoots and cut the onion into wedges about 1-inch long and 1/4-inch thick.

4. Cut the *konnyaku* or zucchini into about 3/4-inch cubes.

5. Cut the chicken into about 1-inch chunks.

6. Heat the oil and sauté chicken until lightly browned. Stir in *dashi* or broth; add carrots, potato or *gobo*, and mushrooms and cook about 10 minutes. Add *konnyaku* or zucchini, onion and bamboo shoots and cook for additional 5 minutes. Add soy sauce, salt and stir well. Stir in peas and cook until they are bright green and just done.

> 1 serving equals: 1 lean meat exchange
>   1 bread exchange
>   123 calories

Cantonese Chicken Chow Mein (Kwang Chaw Gai Chow Mein)*

(Makes 6 servings)

8 oz. of Chinese noodles or thin spaghetti
5 Tbsp. vegetable oil
1/4-inch slice of ginger root, pared
1 cup boned, uncooked chicken, cut into strips
1/4 tsp. salt
2 tsp. light soy sauce
1 tsp. dark soy sauce
1 cup Chinese black mushrooms, washed and cut into strips (canned mushrooms may be substituted)
4 heaping cups Chinese cabbage, sliced into 2-inch strips
1 cup cooked lean ham, cut into strips

1. Cook noodles or spaghetti in boiling water for 15 minutes. Drain under cold water. Add 1 Tbsp. vegetable oil to keep the noodles separated. Set aside.

2. Coat bottom and sides of preheated skillet with 2 Tbsp. oil. Add ginger root, coat bottom and sides, then discard.

3. Quick-fry the chicken, uncovered, for 3 minutes. Add the salt, 1 tsp. light soy sauce and the mushrooms.

---

* Recipe used with the courtesy of: Madame Wu's *Art of Chinese Cooking*, Charles Publishing Company.

4.   Stir in the Chinese cabbage and 1/4 cup water; cover and quick-fry for 5 minutes.

5.   Add the ham, stirring it in thoroughly. Remove chicken and ham mixture to a bowl and set aside.

6.   Preheat the skillet with 2 Tbsp. vegetable oil. Quick-fry noodles for 3 minutes, add the 1 tsp. of dark soy sauce and 1 tsp. light soy sauce. Stir and mix thoroughly.

7.   Add chicken and ham mixture, stir well and serve hot.

> 1 serving equals: 3 medium-fat meat exchanges
> 1 bread exchange
> 1 vegetable exchange
> 312 calories

Chicken with Coconut Milk (Makes 4 servings)

> **4 halves of chicken breasts, boned and skinned**
> **2 Tbsp. shallots, minced**
> **1 cup fresh mushrooms, sliced**
> **1 green bell pepper, seeded, diced**
> **2 Tbsp. vegetable oil**
> **1/4 tsp. curry powder**
> **1/4 tsp. garlic powder**
> **1 cup chicken broth**
> **1 tsp. Worcestershire sauce or soy sauce**
> **Salt and pepper to taste**
> **2 Tbsp. coconut milk**
> **1 Tbsp. cornstarch dissolved in 1/2 cup chicken broth**
> **Sprigs of parsley**

1.   Steam the chicken breasts 20 minutes.

2.   Sauté shallots, mushrooms and green pepper in skillet over medium heat in the vegetable oil until crisp tender, then add curry powder and let cook a few seconds. Keep stirring.

3.   Add garlic powder and blend into mixture, then add 1 cup chicken broth, Worcestershire or soy sauce, coconut milk, salt and pepper. Stir gently.

4.   To the above ingredients add the cornstarch broth mixture, stirring constantly until sauce thickens and is clear.

5.   Place chicken breasts in baking dish. Pour sauce over breasts and cook in 350°F. oven for 30 minutes. Garnish with parsley before serving.

> 1 serving equals: 3 lean meat exchanges
> 1 vegetable exchange
> 190 calories

Cashew Chicken—Iu Kwo Chow Gai Ding* (Makes 4 servings)

2 Tbsp. vegetable oil
1/2 tsp. salt
1 cup sliced chicken breast meat
1/2 cup pea pods
1/2 cup whole button mushrooms
1/2 cup bamboo shoots
1 cup chicken broth
1/2 cup cashew nuts
1/2 tsp. monosodium glutamate (omit if on sodium restriction)
1/2 tsp. cornstarch
1/2 tsp. water

1. Preheat skillet and swirl 2 Tbsp. of vegetable oil around the bottom and sides, sprinkle in salt and quick-fry the chicken for 2 minutes.
2. Add pea pods, mushrooms, bamboo shoots, chicken broth and cover and cook for 2 or 3 minutes.
3. Gently stir in the cashew nuts, monosodium glutamate if used and thicken with the prepared paste of 1/2 tsp. cornstarch and 1/2 tsp. water.

> 1 serving equals: 2 lean meat exchanges
> 1 vegetable exchange
> 1 fat exchange
> 180 calories

Herb-Roasted Chicken (Makes 6 servings)

1 (3-lbs.) whole chicken
1/4 cup parsley
1/2 tsp. sage
1/4 tsp. thyme
1/4 tsp. dill weed
1/8 tsp. rosemary
1-1/2 tsp. coarse salt
1/8 tsp. pepper

1. Heat oven to 400°F.
2. Wash chicken and pat dry.
3. In a small bowl, combine parsley, seasonings, and 1 tsp. salt. Pour this seasoning mix into the chest cavity and shake chicken to distribute.
4. Rub out-side of chicken with remaining 1/2 tsp. of salt.

---

* Recipe used with the courtesy of: Madame Wu's *Art of Chinese Cooking*, Charles Publishing Company.

5. Roast in preheated oven for 1 hour or until chicken is tender and the drumstick moves easily. Serve.

1 serving equals: 3 lean meat exchanges
165 calories

Indonesian Chicken with Coconut Sauce (Makes 6 servings)

3 chicken breasts, skinned, boned, thinly sliced and cut into 1/2-inch strips
Marinade:
3 cloves garlic, smashed and chopped
Juice of 1 lime
2 Tbsp. soy sauce
Sauce:
1/2 tsp. salt
Juice of lime
6 Tbsp. crunchy peanut butter
6 Macadamia nuts, crushed
1 onion, finely chopped
3/4 cup thick coconut milk
1 Tbsp. red chili powder
1 stalk lemon grass, finely chopped
1-1/2 Tbsp. soy sauce

1. In a mixing bowl, thoroughly mix all the marinade ingredients.
2. Thread the chicken strips like a ribbon on six 12-inch wooden skewers, leaving a handle on the blunt end. Place in a large shallow dish.
3. Pour the marinade over the meat and let stand for 45–60 minutes, rotating each stick occasionally.
4. In a saucepan, combine the sauce ingredients and bring to a boil, stirring. Remove from heat and pour into small bowls for dipping.
5. Cook the skewers over charcoals or under broiler.
6. Serve the meat with the sauce.

1 skewer equals: 4 lean meat exchanges
1 fruit exchange
1-1/2 fat exchanges
325 calories

Indonesian Skewered Chicken Grill (Makes 15 skewers)

1 lb. chicken breasts
2 cloves garlic, thinly sliced
2 Tbsp. soy sauce
2 Tbsp. water
Margarine for basting

1. Cut boned chicken breasts into 3/4-inch cubes. Thread 5–6 cubes on each skewer.

2. Mix garlic, soy sauce and water. Dip the threaded chicken pieces into this mixture and grill until meat is done, basting with margarine several times to prevent the chicken from drying out. Turn several times.

3. Serve with peanut sauce.

Peanut Sauce (Makes 1 cup)

> **1 small onion, thinly sliced**
> **1 Tbsp. margarine**
> **1/2 cup water**
> **2 Tbsp. crunchy peanut butter**
> **1/2 tsp. ground chili**
> **Pinch of salt**
> **1/4 tsp. sugar**
> **1 tsp. soy sauce**
> **Juice of half of lemon**

1. Sauté onion in margarine until soft. Add water, peanut butter, ground chili, salt and sugar; stir well.

2. Cook over low heat, stirring constantly, until it thickens. Stir in soy sauce and lemon juice. Check seasoning. Serve on the side with chicken.

> 1 skewer equals: 1 lean meat exchange
> 4 Tbsp. sauce equals: 1 fat exchange
> 100 calories

Chicken and Egg on Rice (Makes 4 servings)

> **4 oz. of chicken, boned, skinned, sliced thin**
> **4 dried mushrooms**
> **Small amount of fresh watercress, cut into pieces 1-inch long**
> **4 eggs, beaten**
> **2 cups cooked rice**
> **4 Tbsp. soy sauce**
> **4 Tbsp. *mirin***

1. Mix soy sauce, *mirin*, and 1-1/2 cups water in a saucepan.

2. Soak the dried mushrooms in warm water, drain, trim off the ends and slice in fine strips.

3. Add chicken and mushrooms to the soy sauce mixture and parboil for 3 minutes.

4. Spread the watercress over the chicken and mushroom mixture.

5. Pour the beaten eggs over the above mixture. Cover the saucepan, turn burner low for 30 seconds.

6. Divide the mixture into four sections and put each portion on top of the rice in individual bowls. Pour the liquid mixture over all and serve.

> 1 serving equals: 2 lean meat exchanges
> 1 vegetable exchange
> 1 bread exchange
> 203 calories

Chicken Omelet over Rice (Makes 2 servings)

> 1/2 chicken breast, skinned, boned, cut into 1/4-inch pieces
> 2 scallions, including about 2-inches of the green stems, cut in half lengthwise,
>   then into 1-1/2-inch pieces
> 1/2 cup *domburi ni shiru* (see recipe below)
> 3 cups steamed rice
> 4 eggs
> Dash of Japanese pepper
> 1 sheet of *nori* (dried seaweed) crumbled

1. Divide the chicken and scallions in half and place them in separate bowls. Mix with 1/4 cup *domburi ni shiru* in each bowl.
2. Place 1-1/2 cups hot steamed rice in each bowl, cover, and keep warm in oven at a low heat while you make the omelets.
3. Pour the contents of one of the bowls of chicken, scallions, and sauce into a 5-inch skillet or crepe pan. Bring to a boil over high heat, reduce the heat to moderate, and cover the pan and cook for 2 minutes.
4. In the meantime, break 2 eggs in small bowl, stir with spoon to combine the yolks and whites. Stir in the pepper and pour the eggs into the pan. Cover pan again and cook another 2 minutes or until the eggs are lightly set.
5. Slice the omelet on top of one of the bowls of rice and garnish with crumbled *nori*.
6. Make second omelet.

> 1 serving equals: 4 lean meat exchanges
> 2 bread exchanges
> 356 calories

Domburi Ni Shiru (Makes 1-½ cups)

> 1/3 cup sweet sake or 1/4 cup pale sherry
> 1/3 Japanese all-purpose soy sauce
> 1 chicken broth

Combine the above ingredients and shake thoroughly.

Pineapple Chicken (Makes 6 servings)

> 3 Tbsp. vegetable oil
> 1 Tbsp. soy sauce
> 1 clove garlic, minced
> 1 tsp. salt
> 1/8 tsp. pepper
> 3 chicken breasts, split
> 3 slices of pineapple, packed in own juice
> 2/3 cup pineapple juice
> 2 Tbsp. cornstarch
> 1 Tbsp. light soy sauce

1. In a large skillet or wok combine oil, 1 Tbsp. soy sauce, garlic, salt and pepper. Add chicken and brown.
2. Add 1/3 cup pineapple juice.
3. Cook over medium heat about 20 minutes or until chicken is tender.
4. Remove chicken to serving platter.
5. Combine cornstarch, another 1/3 cup pineapple juice and 1 Tbsp. soy sauce and add with pineapple chunks to contents of skillet.
6. Cook until thickened. Pour over chicken.

> 1 serving equals: 3 lean meat exchanges
> 1 fruit exchange
> 205 calories

Chicken Pork Adobo* (Makes 10–12 servings)

> 1 chicken, fryer, medium, cut into serving pieces
> 1 pound pork, lean, cut into serving pieces
> 1/2 cup water
> 5 garlic cloves, minced
> 1 tsp. salt
> 10 peppercorn, ground
> 1 bay leaf
> 5 Tbsp. lard
> 2 Tbsp. soy sauce

1. Stew the chicken and pork in a mixture of vinegar, crushed garlic, salt, peppercorn, soy sauce and bay leaf.
2. When the chicken is tender, remove remaining liquid.

* Courtesy of: Mrs. Ma. Patrocinio E. De Guzman, R.D., Clinic Dietitian,Foods and Nutrition Research Center, National Institute of Science and Technology, Republic of the Philippines, Manila.

3. Brown the chicken in lard.

4. Return liquid and cook over moderate heat until sauce is thick.

1 serving (60 grams) equals: 2 medium meat exchanges
2 fat exchanges
246 calories

Red-Cooked Chicken (Makes 6 servings)

2 drumsticks
2 wings
1 back
1 cup chicken broth
1/2 cup soy sauce
2 1/4-inch slices ginger root
3 mashed garlic cloves
2 green onions

1. With a cleaver, chop the wings and drumsticks into 6 pieces, and the back into 6 pieces.

2. Put the pieces of chicken in a small saucepan and cover with the broth and soy sauce, adding more broth or water if needed.

3. Add the rest of the ingredients. Bring to a boil, then simmer for 30–40 minutes.

1 serving equals: 2 lean meat exchanges
1 vegetable exchange
135 calories

Snow Capped Chicken Pie (Makes 6 servings)

3/4 lb. cooked white meat of chicken, ground
2 egg yolks
1 egg
2-1/2 Tbsp. soy sauce
1/2 tsp. salt
3 Tbsp. sake
5 Tbsp. *dashi* ♯2 broth or soup stock
7 Tbsp. minced onion
2 egg whites
5 sprigs of parsley
Oil
Wax paper

1. Place ground chicken in bowl and add soy sauce, salt, sake and chicken

broth.

2.   Beat the egg and egg yolks together and then gradually mix this with the chicken. Mix thoroughly and add the minced onion.

3.   Use a round cake pan. Cut a circle of wax paper to put in the bottom of the cake pan. Lightly oil the paper. Place the chicken mixture into the pan.

4.   Preheat oven to 350°F. Place the chicken pan on top of a baking sheet and bake for 10 minutes.

5.   Beat the egg whites into a stiff foam. Add parsley sprigs.

6.   Remove chicken from oven and top with the beaten egg whites. Return to oven for 2 minutes or until the topping is slightly browned. Cut into wedge shape pieces.

Note: May add 1/2 fat exchange to diet because of the low fat content of the recipe.

> 1 wedge slice equals: 3 lean meat exchanges
> 144 calories

Spicy Chicken with Tangerine (Makes 4 servings)

1/4 cup sake or dry wine
2 Tbsp. soy sauce
1 Tbsp. Chinese or other vinegar
2 whole fryer chicken breasts, skinned and boned
1 Tbsp. soy sauce or other vegetable oil
1 Tbsp. dark sesame oil
Peel of a tangerine or bright skinned orange
4–5 whole, dried hot red chili peppers
1/4 tsp. Szechuan pepper, crushed (optional)

1.   Make a marinade of the wine, soy sauce and vinegar.

2.   Cut the chicken into strips about 1/2-inch by 2-inches, and add to the marinade for 30 minutes or more.

3.   Heat the soy sauce and sesame oil in the skillet; cook the fruit skin and chili peppers for a few minutes. The fruit skin should become slightly scorched.

4.   Drain the chicken and reserve the marinade.

5.   Stir-fry the chicken in the oil for about a minutes, then add the Szechuan pepper and the reserved marinade and cook for about 1 minute longer.

6.   The fruit skin may be eaten, but the hot red peppers should be avoided.

> 1 serving equals: 3 medium-fat meat exchanges
> 219 calories

Chicken Teriyaki (Makes 4 servings)

> **2-1/2 lbs. broiler-fryer chicken, cut up**
> **3/4 cup soy sauce**
> **1/4 cup sugar**
> **1/4 cup dry sherry or white rice wine**
> **2 tsp. grated fresh ginger root**
> **1 small clove garlic, crushed**

1. Wash the chicken in cool water and pat dry with paper towels.
2. Cut the chicken into the desired pieces.
3. Place the cut chicken in a shallow bowl. Combine the soy sauce, sugar, sherry, ginger root and garlic, and pour it over the chicken.
4. Cover and refrigerate for 3 hours, turning occasionally.
5. Drain the chicken, reserving the marinade sauce.
6. Place the pieces, skin side down, in a single layer on a greased 9 × 13-inch baking pan. Bake in 450°F. oven for 10 minutes.
7. Turn chicken and bake 10 minutes more. Reduce the oven temperature to 350°F. Pour off and discard the pan liquid.
8. Continue baking for 30 minutes longer, or until the chicken is tender, brushing 2 or 3 times with some of the reserved marinade.
9. Broil about 6-inches from heat for 3 minutes or until the chicken is well browned.

> 1 serving equals: 4 lean meat exchanges
> 1 vegetable exchange
> 245 calories

Boiled Chicken and Tofu (Makes 4 servings)

> **7 oz. chicken meat, boned, skinned, and cut into 2 pieces per serving**
> **2 cakes of tofu (each cake 2-1/2 × 2-3/4 × 1-inch size), cut into 6 portions**
> **Salt to taste**
> **3 stalks green onions, sliced fine**
> **1 tsp. grated ginger root to get the juice**
> **2 cups soup stock**
> **2 Tbsp. sake or sherry**

1. Add sake to stock, place in pan with chicken meat and tofu, cook over medium heat for 15 minutes.
2. Add soy sauce and salt to taste and bring to boil quickly.
3. Add ginger juice.
4. Divide equally into 4 serving bowls, sprinkle with sliced green onions and serve.

1 serving equals: 2 lean meat exchanges
110 calories

Tomato Pepper Chicken (Makes 4 servings)

8 oz. of chicken breast
2 green peppers
1 Tbsp. vegetable oil
Salt and pepper to taste
1 cup chicken broth
2 Tbsp. cornstarch
1 Tbsp. soy sauce
3 tomatoes

1.   Cook the chicken breast till tender in boiling salted water. Cool and remove the skin and cut the meat into thin strips.

2.   Heat the oil in a skillet or wok and add green peppers cut into strips or squares. Cook gently, with cover on, until pepper is tender. Fast cooking spoils the flavor.

3.   Add salt and pepper and chicken.

4.   Dissolve the cornstarch in a little chicken broth. Add remaining broth to chicken and green pepper and bring to boiling point.

5.   Blend the cornstarch and soy sauce. Stir gently until the sauce thickens, but do not break up the chicken.

6.   Cut tomatoes into wedges and add to the chicken, cooking just enough to heat.

1 serving equals: 3 lean meat exchanges
219 calories

Stir-Fried Chicken with Vegetables (Makes 6 servings)

1 cup raw chicken meat cut from the bones into small pieces
1 green onion, shredded
2 Tbsp. light soy sauce
1 Tbsp. cornstarch
1 Tbsp. sherry
3 Tbsp. peanut oil
1/4 lb. Chinese snow peas, washed, strung, dried
1/4 lb. fresh bean sprouts, washed, dried, sliced
1/4 lb. mushrooms, washed, dried, sliced (may be fresh or canned)
6 water chestnuts, sliced
1/2 cup chicken broth
1 tsp. shredded ginger root

1.   Combine chicken meat, green onion, soy sauce, cornstarch and sherry and let stand, covered, for 1 hour before cooking.

2.   Heat 1 Tbsp. of the oil in a large skillet or wok. Cook the snow peas for 1 minute and remove to a large bowl.

3.   Add another Tbsp. of oil, and when hot, lift the chicken and onion out of the marinade and stir-fry for about 3 minutes then move to one side.

4.   Put in the final Tbsp. of oil and add the water chestnuts and mushrooms.

5.   Return the snow peas to the wok and add the bean sprouts, chicken broth, marinade and ginger root.

6.   Turn heat up high for 1 minute, then turn off heat and serve.

1 serving equals: 1 lean meat exchange
1 vegetable exchange
1 fat exchange
125 calories

Chicken with Vegetables and Curry Coconut Sauce (Makes 4 servings)

4 halves chicken breasts, boned, skinned
Pinch of garlic powder
1 Tbsp. cornstarch
Salt and pepper to taste
2 Tbsp. vegetable oil
1 green bell pepper, cut into small squares
1 medium size onion, diced
4 large stalks celery, diced
1 cup mushrooms, sliced
1 Tbsp. cornstarch dissolved in 1 Tbsp. water
1 cup chicken broth
1 tsp. curry powder
1 orange, unpeeled, cut into wedges
Parsley sprigs

1.   Steam chicken breasts 20 minutes. Set aside. When cool, dust wit. cornstarch, garlic powder, salt and pepper mixture. Heat the vegetable oi. over medium-high heat in skillet, sauté chicken breasts until lightly brown. Set aside.

2.   Steam the vegetables until crisp tender. Set aside.

3.   Add cornstarch and water paste to the chicken broth. Add curry powder and coconut cream, cook over medium heat, stirring until thick and clear.

4.   Spoon steamed vegetables into baking dish or casserole, cover with sauce. Top with chicken breasts. Arrange orange wedges on top of the chicken. Cover casserole with aluminum foil and place in 325°F. oven for 45 min-

utes. Decorate with parsley. Serve.

1 serving equals: 3 lean meat exchanges
2 vegetable exchanges
1 fat exchange
300 calories

Walnut Chicken* (Makes 6 servings)

1 fryer, about 3 lbs., or 1-1/2 lbs. chicken breasts
1 cup walnuts
2 cups vegetable oil
1/3 cup dried mushrooms or 4 oz. canned mushrooms
1/2 cup cubed bamboo shoots
1/4 cup cubed onion
1/2 cup celery
10 water chestnuts
1/3 cup chicken stock or water
Mix:
1 Tbsp. cornstarch
3/4 tsp. salt
3 Tbsp. soy sauce
2 Tbsp. sherry

1. Skin the chicken and remove the meat from the bones. Cut into 1/2-inch cubes and marinate in mixture of cornstarch, salt, soy sauce and sherry.
2. Blanch the walnuts, remove the skins, and deep-fry. Remove and pour off the oil.
3. Wash mushrooms well. Remove the stems and any foreign particles. Soak in water until soft. Squeeze dry and cube.
4. Peel water chestnuts and cube.
5. Heat pan and add 1 Tbsp. oil. Sauté vegetables 1 minute. Remove.
6. Reheat pan, add 2 Tbsp. oil, and sauté chicken 2 minutes. Add vegetables, stock, mix well and cook 2 minutes.
7. Place on platter and garnish with fried walnuts.

1 serving equals: 3 lean meat exchanges
1 vegetable exchange
1 fat exchange
289 calories

---

* Adapted, by permission of the University Press of Hawaii, from Mary Sia's *Chinese Cookbook*, University of Hawaii Press.

Chicken Simmered with White-Radish Threads (Daikon) (Makes 6 servings)

2/3 oz. packaged dried white-radish threads (*daikon*)
2 cups chicken broth or *dashi* #2
3 Tbsp. sugar
1-1/2 tsp. salt
1 Tbsp. all-purpose soy sauce
3 Tbsp. rice wine (sake)
1/2 boned, unskinned chicken breast, cut into 1/2-inch pieces

1.   Wash the *daikon* thoroughly under cold running water, then cover with 2 qts. of cold water in a bowl. Refrigerate for 8–10 hours or overnight.

2.   Drain the *daikon* and transfer it to a 3-qt. pot. Cover with 2 qts. of cold water and bring to a boil over high heat. Lower the heat to moderate and cook uncovered for 2 hours, or until it is tender when pierced with the tip of a sharp knife. Drain in a sieve.

3.   Combine the chicken broth or *dashi*, sugar, salt, soy sauce and rice wine in a 2-qt. saucepan and bring to a boil over high heat.

4.   Add the chicken and *daikon*, and reduce the heat to low. Set a cover smaller than the pan directly on the food, and simmer for 1-1/2 hours. Serve.

> 1 serving equals: 1 lean meat exchange
> 1 vegetable exchange
> 98 calories

Chicken Wings, Peking Style* (Makes 4 servings)

1 lb. chicken wings (8 wings), washed and dried
1 Tbsp. crushed fresh ginger
1 small chili pepper (fresh)
2 Tbsp. sugar
1/2 cup soy sauce
1 star anise
2 tsp. Five Spices seasoning
2 tsp. cornstarch
1/2 cup water
2 Tbsp. sherry
1 Tbsp. oil
4 hard-boiled eggs, shelled

1.   Mix all ingredients together, except chicken wings and eggs.

* Adapted, by permission of the University Press of Hawaii. from Mary Sia's *Chinese Cookbook*, University of Hawaii Press.

2. Bring to boil.
3. Add chicken wings and simmer 15 minutes.
4. Add eggs (whole) and simmer 20 minutes.

1 serving equals: 2 medium-fat meat exchanges
1/2 bread exchange
180 calories

Sautéed Chicken Livers with Garlic (Makes 6 servings)

1-1/4 lb. chicken livers
Salt and freshly ground pepper to taste
1/2 lb. mushrooms
8 Tbsp. vegetable oil
3/4 cup flour
2 Tbsp. margarine
1 Tbsp. finely minced garlic
3 Tbsp. finely chopped parsley

1. Cut away and discard any tough connecting membranes on the chicken livers. Cut the livers into quarters. Put the livers in a bowl and sprinkle with salt and pepper.
2. If the mushrooms are small, leave them whole. If they are large, cut them in half or quarter them.
3. Heat 2 Tbsp. of the oil in a heavy skillet or wok and add the mushrooms. Add salt and pepper to taste. Cook the mushrooms over high heat, shaking and stirring, until they give up their liquid. Continue cooking, stirring, until they are golden brown all over. Drain the mushrooms and set aside. Discard the oil.
4. Add the flour to the livers and stir to coat them well. Place the livers on a baking sheet, separating them.
5. Return skillet to the heat and add 4 Tbsp. oil. When it is quite hot, add half the livers, one at a time. Cook over high heat, turning the livers as they brown. When the livers are cooked, drain thoroughly and transfer them with a slotted spoon to the mushrooms.
6. Add the remaining 2 Tbsp. of oil to the skillet and cook the remaining livers. Drain the livers. Wipe out the skillet.
7. Heat the margarine in a skillet and add livers and mushrooms. Cook, shaking the skillet and stirring, until mixture is hot.
8. Sprinkle the garlic over the liver mixture. Sprinkle this with the parsley. Serve.

1 serving equals: 3 lean meat exchanges
3 fat exchanges
300 calories

or
3 medium-fat meat exchanges
2 fat exchanges
300 calories

Stir-Fried Chicken Livers with Scallops (Makes 4 servings)

1/2 lb. chicken livers, washed and dried
1/2 cup chicken broth
2 Tbsp. soy sauce
1 Tbsp. sherry
2 Tbsp. vegetable oil
3/4 lb. scallops, sliced 1/4" thick
1 thin slice fresh ginger root, minced
2 scallions, minced
1-1/2 tsp. cornstarch dissolved in 1-1/2 Tbsp. water

1.   Place the chicken livers in a bowl and pour boiling water over them. Let stand 3 to 4 minutes. Drain them and dry on paper towels.

2.   Combine the broth, soy sauce, and sherry in a small bowl.

3.   Heat the oil in a large skillet or wok. Add the scallops and stir-fry 2 minutes. Remove them from the pan.

4.   Add the ginger root and scallions and stir-fry 30 seconds. Add the chicken livers and stir-fry 2 minutes.

5.   Pour in the broth mixture and bring to a boil. Stir in the cornstarch mixture and return the scallops to the pan.

6.   Stir just until the scallops are heated through.

1 serving equals: 4 lean meat exchanges
220 calories

Chicken Livers with Vegetables (Makes 6 servings)

1 lb. chicken livers
2 Tbsp. soy sauce
1 Tbsp. sherry
4 stalks celery, cut into 2-inch strips
2 large onions, diced
2 green peppers, seeded and cut into slivers
2 slices fresh ginger root, minced
1 Tbsp. cornstarch dissolved in 1 Tbsp. water
1 cup chicken broth
3 Tbsp. vegetable oil
Salt and pepper to taste

1.   Slice chicken livers into 1/2-inch pieces. Marinate in soy sauce and

sherry for 10 minutes.

2.   In large wok or skillet, heat 1-1/2 Tbsp. of vegetable oil and stir-fry celery strips 1 minute. Add green peppers and onions and stir-fry over high heat until tender crisp. Remove mixture from the pan.

3.   Heat remaining 1-1/2 Tbsp. vegetable oil in skillet. Stir in ginger root for a few seconds. When oil is very hot, add chicken livers, and stir-fry until outside of livers is no longer red. Return the vegetables to the pan and reheat for a few seconds.

4.   Add cornstarch mixture to the chicken broth; then add this to the liver and vegetables, stirring gently until the mixture thickens.

5.   Add salt and pepper to taste. Serve.

> 1 serving equals: 2 lean meat exchanges
> 1 fat exchange
> 145 calories

Duck

Sautéed Curried Duck (Makes 8 servings)

> **1 duck about 5 lbs.**
> **1/4 cup vegetable oil**
> **2 tsp. ground curry powder**
> **4 cloves garlic, minced fine**
> **1/2 cup cider vinegar**
> **1 tsp. salt**
> **1/4 tsp. pepper**
> **1 tsp. brown sugar**

1.   If duck is frozen, thaw completely in the refrigerator. Remove wrappings and cut duck into serving pieces. Dry thoroughly with paper toweling and place in a clean deep bowl.

2.   Heat oil in a skillet. Add curry powder and stir until dark brown. Remove from heat. Add garlic, vinegar, salt, pepper and brown sugar. Stir well. Pour over duck pieces.

3.   Cover tightly and refrigerate for several hours, stirring occasionally to coat duck pieces well.

4.   Pour marinade from duck into a clean skillet; heat until hot. Brown the duck pieces. Turn heat low, cover skillet, and simmer for 3 hours, or until duck is tender. Add a little water if necessary to keep duck from sticking to pan.

> 1 serving equals: 4 lean meat exchanges
> 226 calories

Beef

Beef and Bean Sprouts (Makes 5 servings)

> 1 lb. lean round beef
> 3 Tbsp. vegetable oil
> 1 clove garlic, minced
> 1 tsp. fresh ginger, minced
> 2 cups bean sprouts
> 4 scallions, sliced diagonally
> 2 Tbsp. sherry
> 2 Tbsp. soy sauce
> 1 Tbsp. cornstarch
> 1/2 cup beef broth

1. Slice meat very thin, diagonally across the grain. Pat dry with paper toweling.
2. Heat oil in skillet or wok over medium heat, add beef, garlic and ginger. Stir-fry until just browned. Add sprouts and scallions. Stir.
3. Combine sherry, soy sauce, cornstarch and broth. Add to the beef mixture.
4. Stir and cook for another minute until liquid is thickened and clear.

> 1 serving equals: 3 medium-fat meat exchanges
> 1 fat exchange
> 264 calories

Red-Cooked Beef (Makes 6 servings)

> 1 2-lb. piece of brisket or chuck
> 1 cup soy sauce
> 1 cup chicken broth
> 1 1-inch piece fresh ginger root
> 1 tsp. Five Spices seasoning
> 1 whole piece of anise
> 2 green onions cut in 3-inch pieces

1. Use a saucepan that is just about the size of the beef. Place the beef in the pot and pour the rest of the ingredients over it.
2. If the liquid does not cover, add more chicken broth.
3. Bring to a boil then turn down the heat so the liquid just barely moves.
4. Cook for about 3 hours, depending on the cut.
5. Slice thinly and serve. This dish can be reheated.

1 serving equals: 2 high-fat meat exchanges
1 vegetable exchange
215 calories

Meat Balls in Sauce (Makes 16 meat balls)

3/4 lb. lean ground beef
1/2 onion, diced
2 Tbsp. vegetable oil
1 egg
4 Tbsp. bread crumbs
1/2 tsp. salt
1 tsp. soy sauce
1 Tbsp. sake
Cornstarch
Oil
3 Tbsp. *mirin*
1 Tbsp. soy sauce

1. Over medium heat stir-fry the diced onion in a small amount of the vegetable oil until soft.
2. Mix the beef, onion, egg, crumbs, salt, 1 tsp. soy sauce and sake in a bowl and form into 16 meat balls.
3. Sprinkle the meat balls with cornstarch and fry in the remaining oil over a medium-high heat.
4. In another pan mix the *mirin*, 1 Tbsp. soy sauce and 2 Tbsp. of water, and bring to a boil.
5. Add the meat balls to the *mirin* liquid and shake the pan so the liquid penetrates the meat.

4 meat balls equal: 2 medium-fat meat exchanges
1-1/2 bread exchanges
1 fat exchange
157 calories

Tomato Beef (Makes 4 servings)

1/4 cup soy sauce
2 Tbsp. grated fresh ginger root
2 garlic cloves, minced
1 tsp. cornstarch
1 lb. sirloin tip, thinly sliced
3 Tbsp. vegetable oil
1 lb. medium tomatoes, quartered
4 celery stalks, diagonally cut into 1-inch pieces
6 green onions, cut into 1/2-inch pieces

1 green pepper, cut into 1-inch squares
1 onion, cut into 1/2-inch strips
2 tsp. cornstarch dissolved in 3/4 cup water
1 tsp. soy sauce

1. Combine first 4 ingredients in large bowl. Add meat and marinate at room temperature for 10 minutes. Discard marinade.
2. Heat 2 Tbsp. vegetable oil in large skillet over high heat. When light haze forms, add meat and stir-fry about 2 minutes. Remove with slotted spoon and set aside.
3. Add 1 Tbsp. oil to skillet. When hot, add vegetables and stir-fry until tender crisp. Reduce heat, add dissolved cornstarch mixture, and simmer until thickened. Add soy sauce.
4. Stir in meat and simmer 2 minutes to heat through.

1 serving equals: 2 medium-fat meat exchanges
2 vegetable exchanges
1 fat exchange
241 calories

Noodles with Beef and Chinese Cabbage (Makes 4 servings)

3 Chinese mushrooms, dried and soaked for 30 minutes
6 oz. Chinese cabbage
3 Tbsp. vegetable oil
1/2 cup bamboo shoots, shredded
10 oz. raw beef
1 Tbsp. soy sauce
1 tsp. salt
4 cups cooked egg noodles
1 Tbsp. cornstarch dissolved in 1/2 cup water

1. Slice beef, and marinate with salt and soy sauce for 10 minutes.
2. Cut cabbage into 2-inch lengths. Shred bamboo shoots and mushrooms.
3. In a skillet over medium-high heat, stir-fry the beef in 1 Tbsp. oil. Set aside.
4. Stir-fry the cabbage, mushrooms and bamboo shoots in 2 Tbsp. oil for about 2 minutes.
5. Add the cornstarch mixture. Stir gently until the sauce slightly thickens.
6. Add the cooked noodles, vegetables and beef.
7. Mix well and serve.

Note: You can substitute other meat, such as chicken or pork, for beef. You can substitute other vegetables, such as bean sprouts, green beans, mustard greens, or broccoli, for Chinese cabbage. You can substitute with rice noodles or wheat noodles for egg noodles.

1 serving equals: 2 medium-fat meat exchanges
2 bread exchanges
1 vegetable exchange
2 fat exchanges
397 calories

Tomato Beef* (Makes 4 servings)

1/2 lb. top round steak
2 Tbsp. cornstarch
1 Tbsp. soy sauce
1 Tbsp. brandy
2 Tbsp. peanut oil
1/4 cup chopped onion
1/3 cup celery
3/4 cup green pepper cut in about 1-inch squares
2 whole tomatoes, each cut in 8 sections
1/4 cup sliced water chestnuts
1 cup chicken broth or soup stock, heated
2 tsp. catsup
1/2 tsp. salt
1 tsp. sugar
1 Tbsp. cornstarch mixed with 3 Tbsp. cold water

1. Slice meat about 1/8-inch thick. Mix with cornstarch, soy sauce and brandy. Let stand about 15 minutes while you prepare the rest.
2. Add oil to heated pan; add meat and stir-fry until golden brown; remove and set aside.
3. Add onion and celery. Sauté for about 15 seconds, then add rest of vegetables and stir.
4. Add heated broth, cover and let steam about 1 minute. Remove cover, add meat and mix well.
5. Add seasonings and stir. Thicken slightly with cornstarch mixture.

1 serving equals: 2 medium-fat meat exchanges
1 vegetable exchange
171 calories

---

* Pork or veal may be also be used.

Broiled Sliced Beef with Soy-Seasoned Glaze (Makes 6 servings)

1-1/2 lbs. lean boneless beef, preferably tenderloin or boneless round
1 cup sweet sake or pale dry sherry
1 cup Japanese all-purpose soy sauce
1 cup chicken broth, fresh or canned
1 Tbsp. sugar
2 tsp. cornstarch mixed with 1 Tbsp. cold water
4 tsp. powdered mustard, mixed with a little hot water to make a thick paste
and set aside for 15 minutes to rest
Few sprigs of fresh parsley

1.   Make a sauce by warming the sake over moderate heat in a 1-1/2-qts. enameled or stainless steel saucepan. Turn off the heat and ignite the sake with a match, shaking the pan back and forth until the flame dies out. Stir in the soy sauce and chicken broth and bring to a boil. Pour the sauce into a bowl and cool.

2.   Make a glaze of 1/4 cup of the above sauce and 1 Tbsp. of sugar combined in an enameled or stainless steel saucepan. Bring to a near boil over moderate heat, then reduce to low heat. Stir the combined cornstarch and water paste into the sauce. Cook, stirring constantly, until it thickens into a clear glaze. Pour into a dish and set aside.

3.   Cut the beef into 12 slices 1/4-inch thick. Dip the beef, one slice at a time, into the sauce. Broil the meat 2-inches from the heat until lightly brown or done to desired taste.

4.   When serving, slice the meat into 1-inch wide strips and place on serving dish with a little of the soy-sauce glaze.

5.   Garnish with mustard and parsley.

1 serving equals: 2 lean meat exchanges
110 calories

Spicy Beef and Bean Curd Casserole (Makes 8 servings)

1-1/2 Tbsp. vegetable oil
2 lbs. beef stew meat, cut into 1-inch cubes
1 large onion, cut in half from top to bottom, peeled and cut into 1/4-inch
slices along the grain
2 Tbsp. thin soy sauce
2 Tbsp. sherry or Chinese rice wine
1/4 tsp. sugar
2 cloves garlic, peeled and flattened
1 slice fresh ginger root, 1/8-inch thick, flattened
2 dried chili pepper, broken in half (use both seeds and pods)
2 Tbsp. hoisin sauce
1 Tbsp. ground brown bean sauce

2 Tbsp. vinegar (either cider or distilled white)
1/2 cup chicken broth
2 squares bean curd, cut into 1-inch cubes
2 sweet peppers, stemmed, seeded, deribbed and cut into 1-inch squares
2 tsp. cornstarch
2 tsp. cold water
1/2 tsp. sesame oil

1. Put a large frying pan or skillet over high heat and add enough oil, 1-1/2 Tbsp., to film the pan, tilting the pan to coat the entire surface. When the oil is hot, add beef and onions, and brown turning the pieces often.

2. Mix the braising liquid—soy sauce, sherry, sugar, garlic, ginger root, pepper, hoisin sauce, brown bean sauce, vinegar, and chicken broth—in a 3-qt. casserole.

3. Add the beef and onions to the casserole. Bring the liquid to a boil over high heat. Reduce the heat to medium-low, cover the casserole and simmer for 1 hour.

4. Add the cubes of bean curd and squares of green pepper to the casserole, and simmer the stew another 1/2 hour. Discard the slice of ginger.

5. Mix the cornstarch and water. Stir this mixture into the stew and cook for a few minutes, stirring constantly, until the sauce is slightly thickened.

6. Add the sesame oil, give a final stir, and serve the casserole hot.

> 1 serving equals: 3 medium-fat meat exchanges
> 1 vegetable exchange
> 280 calories

Stir-Fried Beef in Black Bean Sauce (Makes 4 servings)

1/2 lb. flank steak
1 Tbsp. fermented black beans
3 Tbsp. vegetable oil
1 clove garlic, flattened
2 thin slices fresh ginger root, minced
2 small red peppers, cut into strips
1/2 cup chicken broth
1 Tbsp. cornstarch
1 Tbsp. sherry or Chinese rice wine

1. Slice the beef across the grain into very thin slices.

2. Soak the black beans in warm water 10 minutes. Drain, place them in a small bowl and mash with the back of a spoon.

3. Heat two Tbsp. oil in a large skillet. Add the garlic and ginger root, and stir-fry for 1 minute. Remove and discard the garlic.

4. Add the beef and stir-fry for 2 minutes. Remove from the pan.

5. Add the remaining oil to the pan and heat until very hot. Add the

peppers and onion, and stir-fry for 2 minutes. Add the black beans and beef, and stir-fry for 1/2 minute.

6. Pour in the broth and bring to a boil.

7. Dissolve the cornstarch in the sherry or wine and add to the broth mixture. Stir until thickened.

> 1 serving equals: 2 lean meat exchanges
> 2 fat exchanges
> 200 calories

Stir-Fried Ground Round Beef with Vegetables (Makes 6 servings)

> **1 lb. lean ground round beef**
> **1 cup celery, diced finely**
> **1 cup mushrooms, sliced, may be fresh or canned**
> **1 onion, minced**
> **1 green pepper, diced**
> **1 Tbsp. cornstarch**
> **1/2 cup water**
> **2 Tbsp. soy sauce**
> **2 Tbsp. vegetable oil**

1. Brown the beef in heavy skillet, stirring constantly so that the meat is cooked and is in fine particles. Drain off the fat.

2. Push the meat aside in the skillet. Add 2 Tbsp. vegetable oil and cook the celery, mushrooms, onion, and green pepper until done but still crisp.

3. Dissolve the cornstarch in the water. Add the soy sauce. Add this to the meat and vegetable mixture and stir thoroughly.

4. Serve piping hot.

> 1 serving equals: 2 medium-fat meat exchanges
> 1 vegetable exchange
> 171 calories

Beef with Mushrooms (Makes 6 servings)

> **1 clove of garlic**
> **3 Tbsp. vegetable oil**
> **Salt and pepper to taste**
> **1-1/2 lbs. round steak, trimmed of fat, cut in 1/8-inch slices**
> **3 Tbsp. diced onion**
> **1-1/2 cups beef broth or bouillon**
> **1/2 lb. fresh mushrooms, peeled and sliced**
> **3 Tbsp. cornstarch**
> **1 Tbsp. soy sauce**

1.   Place oil and garlic in heavy skillet or wok. Cook gently about 2 minutes and remove garlic.

2.   Add the seasoned steak slices and onion, cooking over a moderate heat, stirring constantly, until the meat is nicely browned. Add the beef broth and sliced mushrooms. Cover the pan tightly and cook gently for about 10 minutes.

3.   Add the soy sauce to the cornstarch with enough water to make a thin paste. Mix well into the broth, cooking over a low heat and stirring constantly until broth thickens.

4.   Serve piping hot.

> 1 serving equals: 3 medium-fat meat exchanges
> 1 vegetable exchange
> 280 calories

Nyrang Rolls* (Makes 1 serving)

3 oz. topside beef steak, thinly cut
1 oz. slice lean bacon
3 slices cut onion rings
10 tsp. beef broth stock
10 tsp. red wine or additional stock
2 tsp. vegetable oil
2 Tbsp. sour cream
Dry mustard
Pepper

1.   Divide meat into 2 pieces. Sprinkle with dry mustard and pepper.
2.   Place bacon (cut in 2 pieces) on meat and top with onion rings.
3.   Roll up and secure with cocktail sticks.
4.   Fry in oil, browning evenly on all sides.
5.   Add liquid and cook in covered frying pan for 1 hour at 300°F.
6.   Reduce liquid to glaze.
7.   Add sour cream and reheat. Serve with boiled rice.

> 1 serving equals: 3 medium-fat meat exchanges
> 1-1/2 fat exchanges
> 1 vegetable exchange
> 1/2 cup cooked rice: 1 bread exchange
> 384 calories

---

* Courtesy of: Mrs. Betty C. Lynch, Chief Dietitian Royal Children's Hospital, Flemington Road, Parkville, Victoria, Australia.

Pork

Pork Dumplings (Makes 48 dumplings)

> **2 cups (about 1 lb.) ground lean pork**
> **1/2 cup minced soaked dried mushrooms or 1/2 cup minced fresh mushrooms**
> **1/3 cup minced green onion**
> **1/4 cup each minced celery, canned water chestnuts, and canned bamboo shoot**
> **2 tsp. minced fresh Chinese parsley or 1/2 tsp. ground coriander**
> **1 tsp. grated fresh ginger root or 1/4 tsp. ground ginger**
> **3 Tbsp. cornstarch**
> **1 egg white**
> **48 fresh or frozen green peas (optional)**
> **Vegetable oil**

1. Stir 1/2 cup boiling water into 1 cup unsifted all-purpose flour, blending thoroughly with a fork.
2. Knead this on moderately floured board for 10 minutes or until very smooth and velvety. Cover for 20 minutes.
3. Roll dough into a log 24 inches-long. When you are ready to fill the dumplings, cut into 1-inch lengths, then cut each section in half to make 48 pieces. Keep covered with plastic.
4. Mix the pork with mushrooms, onion, celery, water chestnuts, bamboo shoots, parsley or coriander and ginger.
5. Gradually blend soy sauce with cornstarch and add to pork mixture along with the egg white. Beat to blend thoroughly. Chill.
6. To make dumplings, roll a piece of dough out on a very lightly floured board to make a 3-inch diameter round. Place a pork ball onto the center of dough. Crumple the dough up and around the filling.
7. Put 1 pea in the center of each dumpling. Brush dumplings all over with vegetable oil. Keep covered and cold until all are shaped.
8. To steam, place slightly apart on a rack, cover, and cook 20 minutes.
9. These may be serve or reheated and served or kept frozen for up to 1 month.
10. To freeze, place slightly apart on a sheet of waxed paper on a baking sheet and freeze until firm, then store in plastic freezer bags. Remove from bags and set dumplings apart to thaw; if they touch, the dough skins stick together. Reheat.

> 4 dumplings equal: 1 medium-fat meat exchange
> 1/2 bread exchange
> 107 calories

Pork Hash and Szechuen Choy (Makes 2 servings)

> 1/2 lb. lean ground pork
> 1/2 cup chopped Szechuen *choy*
> 1/4 cup green onions, cut in 1/4-inch lengths
> 3 Tbsp. soy sauce
> 2 tsp. sugar
> 1-1/2 tsp. sherry
> 1/4 tsp. salt

1. Wash Szechuen *choy* slightly before chopping.
2. Combine all ingredients and mix well.
3. Put in a deep bowl and steam 30 minutes.

> 1 serving equals: 3 medium-fat meat exchanges
> 219 calories

Barbecued Spareribs (Makes 3 servings)

> 2 lbs. spareribs in 1 piece
> 1/4 cup soy sauce
> 2 Tbsp. honey
> 2 Tbsp. white vinegar
> 2 Tbsp. hoisin sauce
> 1 Tbsp. dry sherry or Chinese rice wine
> 1 tsp. finely chopped garlic
> 1 tsp. sugar
> 2 Tbsp. chicken broth

1. Trim off any excess fat from the spareribs. Place ribs in a long shallow dish.
2. Combine the other ingredients, and mix thoroughly. Pour over the ribs and allow to marinate for 3 hours, basting frequently, then drain.
3. Preheat the oven to 375°F. Place the ribs on a rack in a baking pan which contains water to catch the drippings.
4. Roast for 45 minutes, then raise the heat to 400°F. for 15 minutes longer or until the ribs are crisp and a deep brown color.
5. Remove from oven, place on cutting board, and use a cleaver to separate the strips into individual ribs.

Note: The Sweet and Sour Sauce on page 125 may be served with the ribs.

> 1 serving equals: 3 medium-fat meat exchanges
> 219 calories

Spareribs with Black Bean Sauce* (Makes 4 servings)

    1-1/2 lbs. meaty spareribs
    4 Tbsp. peanut oil
    2 large cloves garlic, minced
    1 Tbsp. fresh ginger, minced
    2 Tbsp. black salted soy beans
    2 cups chicken broth
    1 tsp. thin soy sauce
    1 Tbsp. cornstarch dissolved in 1 Tbsp. water
    1 bunch fresh watercress
    Kettle of boiling water

1.   Have the ribs at room temperature and cut them along the meat part into 1-1/2-inch sections.

2.   Peel, then mince or press the garlic and fresh ginger.

3.   Rinse black beans. In a mortar or small cup, mash the garlic, ginger and beans to a paste.

4.   Add the oil to a very hot wok; swirl it around; when it begins to smoke, add the ribs a handful at a time, browning them evenly. After browning, ladle off all but 1 Tbsp. of oil. Add the chicken broth. When it comes to a boil, add the bean mixture and stir until blended. Reduce the heat to medium, cover the wok, and simmer 45–50 minutes. Periodically check the liquid; add more broth if needed to end up with 1/2 cup sauce. Remove the mixture to a saucepan and hold for finishing. You can refrigerate if preparing far ahead.

5.   Bring the ribs to a light boil, stirring to prevent sticking or burning. Correct sauce to 1/2 cup.

6.   Boil a kettle of water. Rinse and pick over the watercress, put it in a colander, pour the boiling water over to wilt it, then put it aside.

7.   When the ribs are hot, take them out of the sauce. Thicken sauce with cornstarch paste, then coat the ribs with sauce.

8.   Place mixture on the serving platter; surround with wilted watercress; serve.

               1 serving equals: 2 high-fat meat exchanges
                                    5 fat exchanges
                                    415 calories
                                    Carbohydrate is negligible.

---

* Recipe courtesy of *Wok Talk*, The Chinese Grocer, San Francisco, Ca. 94108.

Family Style Pork and Bean Curd* (Makes 4 servings)

       1/2 lb. lean pork shoulder or butt
       10 small fresh mushrooms
       2 medium carrots
       3 green onions
       3/4 lb. fresh or canned bean curd
       3 large cloves garlic
       2 slices fresh ginger root
       2 Tbsp. peanut oil
       1/2 tsp. sesame oil
Sauce:
       3 cups chicken stock
       1/2 tsp. dark soy sauce
       1 tsp. "Szechuan" hot bean paste
       1 small dried chili pepper
       1/2 tsp. salt
       2 tsp. cornstarch dissolved in 2 tsp. water

1.   Wash and peel carrots; roll cut. Wash mushrooms and cut hard tips off the stems. Parboil carrots and mushrooms in chicken stock, cool and put aside.

2.   Debone and coarsely chop the pork.

3.   Chop onions into 1/2-inch sections. Slice bean curd into 1-inch blocks. Mince garlic and ginger. Cut dried chili in half. Mix 3/4 cup carrot stock and the other sauce ingredients.

4.   Heat the peanut oil in a hot wok until it begins to smoke, then toss in the pork and stir-fry for 1 minute. Add garlic and ginger; stir-fry for 15 seconds. Add the carrots and mushrooms, then the sauce. Mix together. When the sauce starts to boil, carefully fold in the bean curd, cover, turn down the heat to medium, and simmer for 2 minutes.

5.   Remove cover, turn up the heat. When sauce boils again, stir in the cornstarch paste to make a thick gravy. Cook briefly. Swirl in the sesame oil. Serve.

            1 serving equals: 2 high-fat meat exchanges
                           1 vegetable exchange
                           2 fat exchanges
                           305 calories

---

* Recipe used with the courtesy of *Wok Talk*, The Chinese Grocer, San Francisco, Ca. 94108

Sweet and Sour Pork #1 (Makes 4 servings)

> 6 oz. lean pork
> 3/4 cup bamboo shoots
> 1 tsp. soy sauce
> 1 tsp. salt
> 1/2 egg white
> 1 green pepper
> 1 red pepper
> 2 Tbsp. vegetable oil
> 1 clove garlic, chopped

1. Cut the pork into 1-inch cubes; marinate with salt, soy sauce and egg white for about 20 minutes.
2. Cut the bamboo shoots, green pepper and red pepper into 1-inch squares.
3. Heat 1 Tbsp. vegetable oil in skillet over medium-high heat. Stir-fry pork until almost cooked. Set aside.
4. Stir-fry garlic, bamboo shoots, green pepper and red pepper in 1 Tbsp. vegetable oil for about 1 minute or until tender crisp. Set aside.
5. Combine the pork and vegetables with the Sweet and Sour Sauce and mix well.

> 1 serving equals: 1 vegetable exchange
> 1 medium fat meat exchange
> 1-1/2 fat exchanges
> 163 calories

Sweet and Sour Sauce

> 3 Tbsp. vinegar
> 1-1/2 tsp. cornstarch
> 1 tsp. soy sauce
> Dash of pepper
> 2 Tbsp. catsup
> 3 Tbsp. water
> Artificial sweetener to taste (suggest 1/2 tsp. of liquid artificial sweetener)

1. Combine all ingredients in a small sauce pan.
2. Over medium-high heat, heat the ingredients, stirring constantly until slightly thickened.

This sauce is negligible in calories or exchanges.

Sweet and Sour Pork #2 (Makes 4 servings)

> 1/2 lb. pork shoulder, cut into 1-inch cubes
> 1/2 onion, cut into 1-inch cubes
> 2 green peppers, cut into 1-inch cubes
> 1 carrot, parboiled, cut into 1-inch cubes
> 2 slices canned pineapple (no sugar), cut into 8 pieces
> 8 canned cherries (no sugar), cut into 2 pieces
> Oil for deep-frying plus 4 Tbsp. oil

Mixture (1):

> 1 egg yolk
> 1 tsp. Chinese rice wine or sherry
> 1 tsp. soy sauce
> Salt and pepper to taste
> 1-1/2 Tbsp. cornstarch dissolved in 1 Tbsp. water

Mixture (2):

> 4 Tbsp. catsup
> 3 Tbsp. vinegar
> 2 Tbsp. sugar
> 1 Tbsp. cornstarch
> 2/3 cup water

1. Coat the pork mixture with mixture (1) and let set aside for 1/2 hour.
2. Heat the oil for deep-frying in a wok or skillet.
3. Deep-fry the pork until a golden brown. Remove.
4. Quickly deep-fry the onion, green pepper and carrots. Remove after a few minutes.
5. Heat the 4 Tbsp. of oil in a clean skillet and pour in mixture (2). Stir until the sauce thickens. Add the deep-fried ingredients, mixing them together. Heat through and add the pineapple and cherries.
6. Transfer to serving dish.

> 1 serving equals: 2 lean meat exchanges
> 1 fruit exchange
> 150 calories

Pork and Tofu (Makes 4 servings)

> 1 Tbsp. vegetable oil
> 1 lb. lean pork, cut into 2-inch strips
> 1/3 cup soy sauce
> 1/4 cup sherry
> 1 cup water
> 1 cup tofu
> 1-1/2 cups bamboo shoots
> 2 scallions, including the green tops

1.   Heat the oil in skillet over medium heat. Add the pork and cook, stirring occasionally, until it is lightly browned.

2.   Add soy sauce, sherry and water. Simmer over low heat about 15 minutes.

3.   Cut tofu into 1-1/2-inch cubes. Slice bamboo shoots. Cut the scallions into 1-1/2-inch lengths.

4.   Just before serving, add the tofu and vegetables to the pork mixture and cook until the tofu is heated through.

> 1 serving equals: 3 high-fat meat exchanges
> 2 vegetable exchanges
> 1 fat exchange
> 380 calories

Veal

Veal Sauté Szechuan* (Makes 6 servings)

> 1 lb. veal scallops
> 1 tsp. cornstarch
> 1 Tbsp. thin soy sauce
> 3 cloves garlic
> 1 fresh lemon
> 3 Tbsp. vegetable oil
> 3 dried red chilis (optional)
> Sauce:
> 1-1/2 tsp. sugar
> 1/2 tsp. salt
> 1 Tbsp. dark soy sauce
> 1 Tbsp. sherry
> 1 Tbsp. sesame oil
> 1-1/2 tsp. lemon juice
> 1-1/2 tsp. red wine vinegar
> 1-1/2 tsp. red pepper oil
> 2 Tbsp. chili paste with garlic

1.   Slice veal into thin strips "julienne"; add the soy sauce to the cornstarch; marinate veal in this mixture for 15 minutes.

2.   Slice garlic; crush red chilis. Wash and cut 1 whole lemon, rind and all, into quarters, then into 1/8-inch slices.

3.   Mix the sauce ingredients in a small cup; set aside.

---

* Recipe used with the courtesy of *Wok Talk*, The Chinese Grocer, San Francisco, Ca. 94108.

4. Heat wok or skillet over high heat; add the vegetable oil.

5. When the oil starts to smoke, add the drained veal strips, and stir-fry until they start to color. Remove to the side of the wok.

6. Lower heat slightly, add garlic and stir-fry only until you can smell the garlic. Add lemon slices and sauté very briefly.

7. Push everything back into the center of the wok; add the sauce. Stir until sauce starts to boil. If it is necessary, thicken slightly with cornstarch paste.

1 serving equals: 2 lean meat exchanges
2 fat exchanges
200 calories

Fish and Seafood

Uncooked Fish (Makes 6 servings)

1 large white radish (*daikon*) or 3 cups finely shredded cabbage
1/3 small carrot, peeled
1 lb. very fresh filleted tuna (bluefin or yellowfin), skinned
***Wasabi* paste**
Parsley for garnish
Soy sauce

1. Peel radish and shred into long, fine strands.
2. Shred the carrot the same as the radish.
3. Mix shredded radish and carrot and place in ice water.
4. Rinse fish under cold water, pat dry with paper toweling, cut away and discard any dark portions.
5. Cut fish into slices about 1 to 2-inches wide and 1/8 to 1/4-inch thick.
6. Drain radish-carrot mixture thoroughly and pat dry with paper toweling. Arrange on serving platter.
7. Transfer fish slices to platter in a pleasing pattern.
8. Garnish with parsley.
9. Serve with *wasabi* paste mixed with soy sauce or you may blend until smooth 4 tsp. dry mustard with 3 tsp. water and soy sauce.

Note: Because this fish has a low fat content, 1-1/2 extra fat exchange may be allowed in the diet.

1 serving equals: 3 lean meat exchanges
1 vegetable exchange
120 calories

Kokoda* (Makes 4 servings)

> 1 pound (2 cups) raw tuna, or similar type fish
> Lemon juice, 2 or 3 lemons
> 10 fluid oz. of thick coconut cream made from 3 coconuts with 2 fluid oz.
>   of water
> 1/2 capsicum, small, diced
> 1/2 tomato, chopped, seeds removed
> 2 chilies, chopped
> 1/2 onion, medium, chopped
> Chives, chopped

1.   Skin, clean, and bone the fish. Cut up into even, bite-size pieces (1/2–3/4-inch cubes). Cut straight with a sharp knife. Squeeze out any juice from the flesh of the fish. Place the fish in a bowl and sprinkle with 1–2 Tbsp. salt. Pour on lemon juice. Press the fish well down so that it is covered by lemon juice.

2.   Leave it for at least 1-1/2 hours. Stir occasionally.

3.   When the fish is white and tender, pour off the lemon juice and add the coconut cream to the fish, taste, and add some of the lemon to flavor if necessary.

4.   Chill, and add prepared vegetables just before serving.

5.   This dish is served as part of a buffet-style meal, but it can be prepared on a bed of lettuce as an individual serving.

> 1 serving equals: 2 lean meat exchanges
>   2 fat exchanges
>   Vegetables are free
>   200 calories

Japanese Stew (Makes 4 servings)

> 1/2 lb. cod, raw, cut into bite size pieces
> 12 medium-size shrimp, raw
> Dash of salt
> 16 small-size clams
> Dash of salt
> 1/4 cup dry vermicelli or *harusame* noodles
> 1/2 lb. mushrooms, raw
> 1/4 lb. *enokidake* mushrooms
> 2/3 bunch spinach
> 3 cups *dashi* #2 broth

---

* Recipe courtesy of: Nutrition Department, Fuji School of Medicine, Tamavua Suva, Fuji Islands.

4 Tbsp. Japanese soy sauce
2 Tbsp. *mirin* **or sherry**
1 tsp. salt
4 Tbsp. lemon juice

1.   Place clams to soak in lightly salted water overnight to remove sand. Remove heads from shrimp and devein. Place shrimp in salted water and boil for 2–3 minutes. Remove.

2.   In separate saucepan heat some water to which a little salt has been added and boil the clams until they open. Remove at once and save liquid.

3.   Soak vermicelli until it swells, then cut into 4-inch lengthwise slices.

4.   Remove stems from raw mushrooms, and cut in half if large. Remove stems from spinach and cut leaves into 2-inch lengths.

5.   Add broth to the saved clam liquid to a total of 5 cups. Heat to boiling and add soy sauce, *mirin*, salt. Add all other ingredients and bring to boil.

Note: One extra fat exchange may be allowed in the diet.

1 serving equals: 1 lean meat exchange
2 bread exchanges
146 calories

Steamed Fish with Noodles (Makes 4 servings)

12 oz. of fillet of white fish
2 oz. of dried thin noodles
2 Tbsp. soy sauce
2 Tbsp. sweet sake or dry sherry
3/4 cup reconstituted dried soup stock or liquid chicken broth
1/8 tsp. monosodium glutamate (omit if on sodium restriction)
Parsley for garnish; radishes for flower

1.   Cut the fish fillet into 4 portions. Make a lengthwise cut to within 1/2-inch of the far edge of each portion. Salt lightly.

2.   Boil the noodles until tender. Drain, rinse with cold water and drain thoroughly.

3.   Divide the noodles into 4 portions, and wrap a portion in each of the fillets.

4.   Arrange the fish in serving bowls (4) and pour 2 tsp. of sake or sherry over each fillet.

5.   Set the bowls on rack or steaming basket and place over boiling water. Steam for 10–12 minutes.

6.   Mix the other ingredients for a sauce in a small saucepan. Bring to a boil and pour over the fish before serving.

7.   Garnish each bowl with a radish flower and parsley.

$$1 \text{ serving equals:} \quad 3 \text{ lean meat exchanges}$$

1 serving equals: 3 lean meat exchanges
1/2 bread exchange
199 calories

Broiled Fish and Mushrooms (Makes 6 servings)

8 oz. mushrooms
6 large shrimp, cooked and deveined
12 oz. white meat fish, cut into bite size pieces
1 cup water chestnuts (boiled or canned)
3-1/2 oz. gingko nuts
2 Tbsp. sake
Lemon juice
6 squares, 9-inch by 9-inch, aluminum foil

1.   Sprinkle the mushrooms, shrimp and white fish meat with a little sake and salt.
2.   Place the above, divided equally, in the center of a sheet of aluminum foil.
3.   Add chestnuts, sprinkle with 1 tsp. sake, and wrap each square.
4.   Place foil-wrapped ingredients in heated frying pan, cover and broil over medium heat for about 7 minutes.
5.   When cooked, place on plate and serve with lemon juice.

1 serving equals: 1 lean meat exchange
1 bread exchange
123 calories

Fried Flounder with Peppers (Makes 4 servings)

1 lb. flounder fillets or substitute any firm white fish
2 thin slices fresh ginger root, minced
1/2 tsp. salt
1/2 tsp. vegetable oil
1 Tbsp. sherry
1 egg, lightly beaten
1 Tbsp. cornstarch
5 Tbsp. vegetable oil
1 thin slice fresh ginger root
1 clove garlic
1 small red pepper, cut into small diamond shapes
1 small green pepper, cut into small diamond shapes
1 medium size onion, cut lengthwise into strips
1 tsp. sherry
1 tsp. soy sauce

1. Cut the fish fillets across the grain into 1-1/2-inch pieces.
2. In a bowl, combine the minced ginger root, salt, 1/2 tsp. of oil and the sherry.
3. Add the fish and toss to coat. Let stand 2 hours, tossing occasionally. Drain the fish and dry thoroughly.
4. Dip each piece in egg and sprinkle evenly with cornstarch.
5. Heat 1 Tbsp. oil in a large skillet or wok. Add the slice of ginger root and garlic and brown lightly. Remove and discard garlic and ginger root.
6. Add the peppers and onion and stir-fry for 2 minutes. Mix in the sherry and soy sauce, and remove the ingredients from the pan.
7. Add the remaining oil and heat until very hot. Add the fish and fry quickly until golden brown on both sides.
8. Drain on paper towels and arrange on a serving plate.
9. Garnish with peppers and onion and serve.

> 1 serving equals: 4 lean meat exchanges
> 1 vegetable exchange
> 245 calories

Fish Teriyaki (Makes 6 servings)

> **1 cup soy sauce**
> **1/2 cup sugar**
> **1/4 cup salad oil**
> **2 tsp. grated fresh ginger root**
> **1 clove garlic, chopped (optional)**
> **2 lb. rockfish fillets**
> **1 Tbsp. sesame seeds**

1. In a bowl, combine soy sauce, sugar, oil, ginger and garlic.
2. Let the fillets stand in this mixture for several hours.
3. Lift the fillets from the soy sauce mixture and arrange in a shallow pan that has been lined with aluminum foil.
4. Broil 5 to 7 inches from the heat for about 4 minutes, brushing with a little oil. Turn, brush with more oil, and sprinkle with sesame seeds.
5. Broil 3 to 5 minutes longer or until the fish flakes.

> 1 serving equals: 3 lean meat exchanges
> 165 calories

Fish and Tofu Stew (Makes 4 servings)

> **4 cups _dashi_ ♯1 (soup stock)**
> **1 lb. of cod fillets**

3/4 lb. tofu
4 dried mushrooms
2 leeks, chopped
1/2 tsp. lemon juice
1 tsp. soy sauce
1/4 tsp. monosodium glutamate

1. Soak the mushrooms in a small amount of water to soften. Slice lengthwise.
2. Cut the fish into bite-size pieces.
3. Dice the tofu.
4. Bring the soup stock to a boil.
5. Add the fish, mushrooms and tofu. Bring to boil, then turn the heat to low and allow the mixture to simmer for about 20 minutes.
6. Make a sauce of the chopped leeks mixed with lemon juice and soy sauce. Serve with the stew.
7. Serve in individual bowls.

1 serving equals: 4 lean meat exchanges
220 calories

Baked Sole with Seafood Topping (Makes 8 servings)

3 Tbsp. vegetable oil
8 small sole fillets
Salt, freshly ground pepper to taste
Topping:
1/4 cup vegetable oil
1/2 cup white onion, chopped
1/2 cup celery, chopped
1/2 cup shallots, chopped
1/4 cup green pepper, chopped
1 garlic clove, pressed
1 Tbsp. cornstarch
1/2 cup white wine
1/2 cup non-fat milk
1/2 cup boiled shrimp, chopped
1/2 lb. lump crab meat shredded
1/2 cup bread crumbs
2 Tbsp. chopped fresh parsley
1 egg, lightly beaten
Salt, freshly ground pepper, cayenne to taste

1. Grease shallow baking pan with 1 Tbsp. oil.
2. Brush fish with 2 Tbsp. oil, season with salt and pepper, and place in a baking dish.

3.   Topping: heat oil in skillet over medium-high heat. Add onion, celery, shallot, green pepper, garlic and sauté until tender. Blend in cornstarch. Add wine and milk and stir until thickened. Remove from heat.

4.   Add next 5 ingredients and mix well. Season with salt, pepper, cayenne.

5.   Top fillets with the topping. Cover baking dish and bake in 375°F. oven for 25 minutes. Remove cover and bake 5 minutes longer to brown.

> 1 serving equals: 4 medium-fat meat exchanges
> 1 vegetable exchange
> 317 calories

Steamed Cod with Mushrooms in Sweet Vinegar Sauce*
(Makes 4 servings)

> 3/4 lb. filet of cod, fresh or frozen
> 2 Tbsp. peanut oil
> 1 medium size carrot
> 8 *Nami* black mushroom
> 1 cup warm water
> 3/4 cup sliced fresh mushrooms
> 2 cloves garlic
> 1 tsp. minced ginger root
>
> Sauce:
> 2/3 cup chicken broth
> 1/3 cup mushroom soaking liquid
> 1 Tbsp. Chinkiang vinegar
> 2 tsp. crushed rock sugar
> 1/4 tsp. sesame oil
> 2 tsp. cornstarch dissolved in 2 tsp. water

1.   Thaw frozen fish, bring to room temperature, pat and thoroughly dry.

2.   Wash and soak *Nami* mushrooms in warm water for 1 hour. Slice carrot into thin rounds. Squeeze soaking liquid from mushrooms; reserve liquid; slice *Namis* thinly. Slice fresh mushrooms the same way. Peel and mince the garlic and the ginger root.

3.   In a small saucepan, heat peanut oil to moderate; sauté the sliced vegetables and garlic for 1 minute. Add the sauce ingredients, *except* the sesame oil and cornstarch paste. Bring to a boil, then reduce heat and simmer, covered, for 10 minutes. Just before serving, bring back to a gentle boil, dribble in the cornstarch paste, stirring until the sauce thickens.

4.   Sprinkle the fish with minced ginger, and steam for 8–10 minutes, until it just turns white all the way through.

* Courtesy of: *Wok Talk*, The Chinese Grocer, San Francisco, Ca. 94108.

5. Remove fish from steamer, pour off accumulated water. Pour the sauce over fish, sprinkle with sesame oil, and serve.

> 1 serving equals: 2 lean meat exchanges
> 1 vegetable exchange
> 135 calories

Steamed Sea Bass with Scallions (Makes 6 servings)

1 2-lb. sea bass
1-1/4 tsp. salt
1 tsp. monosodium glutamate (omit if on sodium restriction)
2 Tbsp. wine
4 slices ginger, finely chopped
6 scallions
1/4 tsp. pepper
1 tsp. sesame oil
2 tsp. peanut oil
2 Tbsp. chicken stock
1 Tbsp. soy sauce
Parsley for garnish

1. Clean the fish and rub with the combined mixture of 1 tsp. salt, 1/2 tsp. monosodium glutamate (if used), 2 Tbsp. wine and half of the chopped ginger.
2. Shred the scallions.
3. Place the fish in the steamer, steam over high heat for about 10 minutes, then remove. Sprinkle 1/4 tsp. black pepper and 1 tsp. sesame oil over the fish.
4. Heat the peanut oil over high heat until it is smoking, then add the scallion and the remaining ginger shreds.
5. Remove them from the oil and sprinkle over the fish.
6. Boil the chicken stock seasoned with the soy sauce, the remaining salt and monosodium glutamate (if used), and pour over fish.
7. Garnish with parsley and serve.

> 1 serving equals: 3 medium-fat meat exchanges
> 219 calories

Ocean Swell (Makes 6 servings)

7 oz. canned crab meat
7 oz. canned bonita
2 hard-cooked eggs, diced
1 tsp. tarragon flakes

2 Tbsp. lemon juice
3 eggs, separated
1/2 cup non-fat milk
1/2 tsp. salt
1/2 tsp. celery salt
Dash cayenne

1. Heat oven to 350°F.
2. Remove membrane from crab meat; drain bonita and break into flakes.
3. Mix seafood with egg, tarragon flakes and lemon juice.
4. Beat egg yolks until thick and lemon-colored. Blend in milk and seasonings. Add fish mixture and mix well.
5. Beat egg whites until stiff but not dry. Fold into egg-fish mixture.
6. Pour into a 1-1/2-qt. greased casserole or baking dish.
7. Bake in 350°F. oven for 1 hour or until set.

1 serving equals: 2-1/2 lean meat exchanges
135 calories

Savory Crab Meat in Sauce (Makes 4 servings)

3 Tbsp. vegetable oil
1/3 cup finely diced onion
1/3 cup finely diced green pepper
1/3 cup finely diced celery
3 Tbsp. cornstarch
1-1/4 cups chicken broth
1/3 cup finely diced pimento
Juice of 1/2 lemon
1 Tbsp. parsley flakes
Dash of soy sauce (light)
Salt and freshly ground pepper to taste
1 tsp. Five Spices seasoning
1-1/2 cups flaked crab meat
Watercress for garnish

1. Heat vegetable oil in skillet or wok over medium-high heat.
2. Add onion, pepper, celery and sauté for 1 minute.
3. Sprinkle with cornstarch, stirring constantly, until well blended.
4. Gradually add broth, stirring until sauce is smooth and thickened.
5. Blend in pimento, lemon juice, parsley flakes, salt, pepper and Five Spices seasoning.
6. Add crab meat and cook for 10 minutes, stirring gently.
7. Garnish with watercress when served.

1 serving equals: 1 medium-fat meat exchange
1 vegetable exchange
1 fat exchange
143 calories

Crab Meat with Mushrooms (Makes 5 servings)

8 oz. straw mushrooms
1/4 lb. crab meat
1/4 tsp. salt
Dash of pepper
2 Tbsp. vegetable oil
Gravy:
1/2 tsp. cornstarch
1 Tbsp. oyster sauce
1/8 tsp. sesame oil
1 egg white
5 Tbsp. water or chicken broth

1. Marinate the crab meat with salt and pepper for 10 minutes.
2. Heat oil in skillet over medium heat and stir-fry the mushrooms.
3. Add crab meat. Stir-fry for 1 minute. Set aside.
4. Combine the ingredients for the gravy in a saucepan and cook over a medium heat, stirring constantly, until slightly thickened.
5. Pour the gravy over the mushrooms and crab meat mixture, and serve.

Note: You can substitute other meat such as chicken, minced meat or shrimp for the crab.

1 serving equals: 1 medium-fat meat exchange
1 vegetable exchange
98 calories

Steamed-Broiled Shrimp, Chicken, Mushrooms (Makes 4 servings)

4 shrimp, medium size
4 mushrooms, medium size
12 gingko nuts
1 whole chicken breast, boned, skinned, cut into bite-size pieces
8 large chestnuts
Coarse salt
Pine needles

1. Shell shrimp and devein. Wipe mushrooms with damp cloth.
2. Using 4 small bamboo skewers, thread an equal number of gingko nuts on each. Do the same with the boned cut chicken.

3. Preheat oven to 400°F. Using a sharp knife, make a deep cross on each chestnut. Place these on a baking sheet and bake in oven for 10 minutes.

4. Pour a 1/2-inch layer of coarse salt into a 12 to 14-inch unglazed earthernware casserole. Sprinkle a few drops of water over the salt. Place casserole over moderate heat for 5 to 10 minutes or until the salt is heated through.

5. Arrange pine needles on the salt bed. Place shrimp, mushrooms, skewered chicken and chestnuts on top of pine needles. Scatter a few pine needles on top of the food. Cover casserole tightly with aluminum foil and steam over moderate high heat for 15 minutes.

6. Remove top pine needles and serve food with sauce.

> 1 serving equals: 2 lean meat exchanges
> 1 vegetable exchange
> 135 calories

Spicy Sauce for Steamed-Broiled Shrimp (Makes 1 cup)

> 2 Tbsp. sake
> 1/4 cup *daikon*, shredded
> 2 scallions, sliced
> 1/4 cup Japanese all-purpose soy sauce
> 1/4 cup lemon juice
> 1/8 tsp. seven-pepper spice

1. Warm sake in small saucepan. Turn off heat, ignite sake with a match, shake pan gently until flame dies out. Pour sake into small dish to cool.

2. In a mixing bowl combine sake and grated *daikon*, sliced scallions, soy sauce, lemon juice and spice. Mix well.

3. Serve in individual bowls.

Sauce may be used without an exchange value.

Crab with Vegetables (Makes 4 servings)

> 1 cup canned, fresh or frozen crab meat, flaked
> 2 Tbsp. vegetable oil
> 1/4 cup green onions, sliced diagonally
> 6 water chestnuts, thinly sliced
> 2 carrots, thinly sliced diagonally
> 6 oz. snowpea pods, fresh or frozen (thawed)
> 1/2 cup chicken broth
> 1/4 cup dry sherry or dry white wine
> 2 Tbsp. soy sauce
> 1 Tbsp. cornstarch

1. Steam the crab meat (thaw first if frozen), drain and break into pieces.
2. Heat oil in skillet or wok over medium-high heat.
3. Add green onions, water chestnuts, carrots and pea pods, and stir-fry till crisp tender.
4. Combine chicken broth, sherry, soy sauce and cornstarch.
5. Add the chicken liquid to the vegetable mixture; stirring constantly. Cook until sauce is slightly thickened.
6. Add crab meat, stir mixture gently until thoroughly heated, and serve.

1 serving equals: 1 lean meat exchange
1/2 fat exchange
2 vegetable exchanges
125 calories

Seafood* (Makes 4 servings)

2-1/2 oz. spinach leaves
8 pods okra
2 cups water, boiling
1 crab
1 tomato, sliced
1 onion
2 oz. of salt meat or ham bones
1 tsp. lemon juice
1 Tbsp. lard
1 clove garlic
Salt and pepper

1. Strip the spinach leaves and wash well.
2. Clean the crab thoroughly, cut up the meat.
3. Wash and slice the okra.
4. Cup up the tomato and onion.
5. Place all ingredients in pot, add boiling water and simmer until soft.
6. Stir and add lard or margarine.
7. This can be served as a soup or as a vegetable dish.

1 serving equals: 1 lean meat exchange
1 vegetable exchange
80 calories

---

* Courtesy of: Julia O. Rose, Nutritionist, Woodbrock, Port of Spain, Trinidad, West Indies.

Seafood and Scallions in Miso Dressing (Makes 6 servings)

1 lb. cleaned fresh squid or 18 shucked clams plus 1 cup clam juice
1/2 tsp. salt
8 scallions, including the green stems, trimmed and cut into 1-1/2-inch lengths
3 Tbsp. rice vinegar or mild white vinegar
1/3 cup white miso dressing (page 125)
1 Tbsp. powdered mustard, mixed with a little hot water to make a paste

1.   Under cold running water, peel off and discard the lacy outer membrane of the squid. Pat dry with paper towels, slice in half lengthwise without cutting completely apart, spread open, butterfly fashion. Cut the squid lengthwise in 1/8-inch wide strips.

2.   Boil 2 cups of water in small saucepan. Add the strips of squid and return the water to boil. Drain at once, rinse with cold water and set aside.

3.   Bring 2 cups water to boil, add the salt and drop the scallions into the boiling water for 1 minute. Drain at once and run cold water over them to cool quickly.

4.   In a mixing bowl, stir the vinegar and miso dressing, then add the mustard paste. Mix until smooth.

5.   Add the scallions and squid to the miso dressing and stir gently until thoroughly mixed.

6.   If you use clams, save the juice. Strain the clam juice through a fine sieve into a small saucepan and bring to boil over high heat. Add the clams, return to a boil, then drain and set aside to cool. Slice the clams into narrow strips.

1 serving equals: 2 lean meat exchanges
1/2 bread exchange
144 calories

Broiled Scallops (Makes 4 servings)

16 fresh scallops
2 tsp. melted butter or margarine
Juice of 1 lemon
Freshly ground pepper to taste
1 tsp. parsley flakes
Soy sauce

1.   Place scallops on broiler: brush on melted butter mixed with lemon juice.

2.   Sprinkle scallops with pepper.

3.   Broil scallops until done.

4. Sprinkle with soy sauce and parsley flakes.

> 1 serving equals: 1 lean meat exchange
> 55 calories

Stir-Fried Scallops (Makes 3 servings)

> 1/2 lb. scallops
> 3 cloves galic
> 1/2-inch piece of fresh ginger
> 3 Tbsp. vegetable oil
> 2 large stalks celery, sliced
> 1-1/2 Tbsp. black bean sauce
> 2 Tbsp. soy sauce
> 1/4 tsp. red pepper powder or to taste
> 1/4 lb. fresh mushrooms, sliced
> 3 scallions, cut in 1/2-inch pieces, including green tops
> 5 water chestnuts, sliced

1. Cut scallops into 2 pieces each.
2. Cut garlic and ginger to match-head-size pieces.
3. Heat the oil in wok or skillet over medium heat. When oil is hot, add garlic and ginger. Stir-fry 30 seconds.
4. Add celery and cook for 30 seconds longer.
5. Add scallops and stir-fry for 1 minute. Add black bean sauce, soy sauce and red pepper. Stir-fry for 1 minute.
6. Add mushrooms, scallions and water chestnuts, and cook for 2 minutes longer, then serve.

> 1 serving equals: 2 lean meat exchanges
> 1 vegetable exchange
> 1 fat exchange
> 190 calories

Shrimp with Peas (Makes 4 servings)

> 1 lb. raw shrimp in shells
> 1 lb. fresh peas or 1 cup frozen peas
> 2 tsp. cornstarch
> 1 egg white
> 2 tsp. pale dry wine or Chinese rice wine
> 1 tsp. salt
> 1 Tbsp. vegetable oil
> 1 scallion, including the green top, cut into 2-inch lengths
> 3 slices peeled fresh ginger root (1 inch in diameter and 1/8-inch thick)

1.   Shell and devein the shrimp with a sharp knife. Wash the shrimp under cold water and pat dry with paper toweling.

2.   Split the shrimp in half lengthwise, then cut each of the halves in two, lengthwise.

3.   Drop the peas (shelled) in boiling water; cook uncovered for 7 minutes. The frozen peas need only to be defrosted.

4.   Combine the shrimp and cornstarch in a large mixing bowl, toss lightly with a spoon until each shrimp is coated with the cornstarch.

5.   Add egg white, wine and salt, and stir them with the shrimp until thoroughly mixed.

6.   Heat skillet for 30 seconds, add oil and swirl this around the skillet and heat for 30 seconds. Turn heat down if the oil begins to smoke.

7.   Add scallions and ginger, stir-fry for 30 seconds to flavor the oil, then remove with slotted spoon and discard. Drop in the shrimp and stir-fry for 2 minutes or until they turn pink. Do not overcook.

8.   Add peas and stir-fry for 1 minute.

> 1 serving equals: 3 lean meat exchanges
> 1 vegetable exchange
> 190 calories

Butterfly Shrimp with Snow Peas, Straw Mushrooms and Water Chestnuts (Makes 4 servings)

> **1/4 lb. of fresh or frozen shrimp, medium sized**
> **1-1/2 cups fresh or frozen snow peas**
> **9 large fresh or canned water chestnuts**
> **1/2 cup unpeeled straw mushrooms (may use canned mushrooms)**
> **2 tsp. fresh ginger, slivered**
> **1 large clove garlic, minced**
> **2 green onions**
> **3 Tbsp. vegetable oil**
> **1/2 cup chicken stock or broth**
> **2 tsp. thin soy sauce**
> **1 tsp. dry sherry**
> **1/2 tsp. salt**
> **1 Tbsp. cornstarch dissolved in a little water**

1.   Soak snow peas in cold water for 2 hours to make them crisp.

2.   Soak shrimp in salted cold water for 1 hour.

3.   Drain mushrooms.

4.   Break off ends of snow peas. Peel and rinse water chestnuts. Shell shrimp, keeping tail intact. Deeply slit the shrimp around the curve (do not cut through), taking out the black vein; spread the shrimp almost flat.

5.   Sliver ginger; mince garlic. Cut green onion on the bias in 2-inch

lengths. Slice water chestnuts thinly crosswise. Place ingredients in separate piles on the serving platter.

6. In small bowl, mix liquid ingredients.

7. Swirl vegetable oil in very hot skillet or wok. When oil begins to smoke, add shrimp and stir-fry until they curl (about 20 seconds).

8. Remove shrimp to serving platter.

9. Stir-fry mushrooms for 30 seconds, then add garlic and ginger; stir-fry another 30 seconds.

10. Add snow peas and water chestnuts; stir-fry briskly for 1 minute.

11. Add stock mixture, bring to boil; keep tossing until snow peas are bright green.

12. Push ingredients out of liquid; dribble in the cornstarch paste to thicken.

13. Return ingredients, including shrimp. Stir briefly. Serve at once.

14. Snow peas should be slightly undercooked when served; do not cover the skillet or wok.

>
> 1 serving equals: 1 lean meat exchange
> 1 fat exchange
> 1 vegetable exchange
> 125 calories

Mandarin Shrimp (Makes 6 servings)

> **2 Tbsp. vegetable oil**
> **1 clove garlic, crushed**
> **1/2 tsp. ginger**
> **Salt and pepper**
> **2 lbs. fresh shrimp**
> **3/4 cup water**
> **3/4 cup catsup**
> **1 Tbsp. cornstarch**
> **Water**
> **Rice, cooked, 3 cups**

1. Crush clove of garlic in oil and cook very gently for 3–4 minutes. Remove the garlic and add other seasonings and blend.

2. Add the shelled, cleaned shrimp to the oil and cook, stirring gently, for 3 minutes. Add water, cover tightly and cook for 5 minutes uncovered.

3. Make a paste of the cornstarch and a little water to thicken the juices.

4. Serve over hot rice.

>
> 1 serving equals: 3 lean meat exchanges
> 1/2 cup cooked rice: 1 bread exchange
> 233 calories

Sunchoke and Shrimp Stir-Fry (Makes 8 servings)

> **8 green onions, chopped with tops**
> **1 green pepper, sliced thin**
> **1/2 lb. mushrooms, sliced**
> **3 cups cooked rice (wild rice is delicious)**
> **1 cup scrubbed, peeled, sliced sunchokes (Jerusalem Artichokes)**
> **1 lb. cooked shrimp**
> **2 Tbsp. cooking oil**
> **4 Tbsp. margarine or butter**
> **1/4 cup parsley, chopped**
> **1 Tbsp. soy sauce**

1. Heat oi! and margarine in a skillet and sauté the onions for about 2 minutes. Add the green pepper, continue stirring and toss in the mushrooms. Cook 2–3 minutes.
2. Add the rice, shrimp, and sunchokes. Cook, stirring to heat through.
3. Toss in the parsley and season with soy sauce.

Note: You may substitute lobster or crab for the shrimp.

> 1 serving equals: 1 lean meat exchange
> 1 bread exchange
> 1 vegetable exchange
> 1 fat exchange
> 193 calories

Tempura

Tempura Coating (Makes 1-⅔ cups)

> **2 eggs**
> **15 Tbsp. (1 cup minus 1 Tbsp.) cold water**
> **3/4 cup unsifted flour**
> **1/2 tsp. salt**

1. Beat the eggs with the cold water until frothy.
2. Add the flour and salt and beat until blended—do not beat the flour any more than is necessary.
3. Set the bowl of batter in the refrigerator to keep cold until used.

> 1/4 cup batter equals: 1 bread exchange
> 68 calories

Tempura (Makes 4 servings)

> **8 shrimp**
> **8 small white fish or 8 slices of fish 2 oz. per slice**
> **4 small eggplants**
> **8 small green peppers**
> **1 kernel ginger root**
> **Coating—see page 115**
> **Sauce—see page 117, allow 1/4 cup per serving**

1.   Remove the shells from the shrimp leaving the tails on. Clean and stretch them out straight so that they will not curl while cooking.
2.   If the white fish are small, leave the tails on while cleaning and remove the bones. Remove the skin and bones and fillet the flesh into 1 oz. slices if flounder or sea bass is used.
3.   Cut the eggplant into 1/2-inch thick slices.
4.   Cut the green peppers in half lengthwise and remove the seeds.
5.   Peel the ginger root and cut into 1/4-inch thick slices.
6.   Dip the food items in the tempura batter and fry quickly in hot oil for 2 minutes. Place the cooked foods on a screen to drain the oil off.
7.   Dip the cooked food in tempura sauce. If desired, the tempura can be eaten with salt and lemon.

> 1 serving of 2 shrimp and 4 oz. of fish and vegetables
> equals: 2 lean meat exchanges
> 2 vegetable exchanges
> 1 bread exchange
> 1 fat exchange
> 173 calories

Tempura—Shrimp and Vegetables (Makes 4 servings)

> **12 large shrimp**
> **8 scallops**
> **Vegetables:**
> **2 carrots**
> **2 green peppers**
> **1 medium size eggplant**
> **Tempura Coating—page 115**

1.   Shell the shrimp, leaving the tail fins attached to the flesh; remove the black veins. Slit undersection of shrimp to prevent excessive curling. Wash shrimp thoroughly.
2.   Cut the scallops in slices and wash thoroughly.
3.   Wash vegetables and remove the seeds from the green peppers.

4. Cut the vegetables into fine strips.

5. To cook, dip shrimp and scallops into tempura coating and fry in very hot oil for 3 minutes. Drain on paper toweling.

6. Dip the vegetables in tempura coating. Fry in hot oil for 1 minute.

7. Arrange on a serving platter.

1 serving equals: 1 lean meat exchange
1 vegetable exchange
1 fat exchange
125 calories

Tempura Sauce (Makes 5 cups)

> 3 cups *dashi* or fish stock
> 1 cup soy sauce
> 1 cup *mirin* (sweet rice wine)

1. Combine the above ingredients in a pan and bring to a boil; remove from the heat.

2. Serve hot in individual bowls.

1/4 cup sauce equals: 1 vegetable exchange
25 calories

Salads

Bean Sprouts Salad (Makes 4 servings)

> 1 lb. fresh bean sprouts (soybean or mung bean)
> 1 recipe dressing:
>   2 Tbsp. soy sauce
>   4 tsp. lemon juice
>   1 Tbsp. sesame oil
>   1/2 tsp. salt

1. Bring 2 qts. of water to a boil; remove from the heat.

2. Add the bean sprouts to the hot water and let stand for 1 minute.

3. Drain the hot water and add cold water, letting the sprouts stand in the cold water until they have cooled.

4. Drain thoroughly and set aside.*

---

* If canned bean sprouts are used, blanching is not necessary.

5. Combine the dressing ingredients and mix well.

6. Pour the dressing over the bean sprouts and serve.

> 1 serving equals: 2 vegetable exchanges
> 50 calories

Celery and Crab Salad (Makes 4 servings)

> **2 stalks celery**
> **1/4 lb. crab meat (canned), boned and shredded**
> **5 small cucumber, thinly sliced laterally**
> **Salt**
> **Vinegar-soy-sauce dressing**
> **1 cup vinegar**
> **1 tsp. soy sauce**
> **Artificial sweetener equal to 3 Tbsp. sugar**

1. Remove stringy part of celery, cut into 2-inch lengths, slice fine length-wise and soak in water 10 minutes. Drain.

2. Sprinkle cucumber slices with salt, work in salt with fingers and drain by compressing with hands.

3. Mix all vinegar-soy-sauce dressing ingredients thoroughly.

4. Combine celery, crab meat, and cucumber slices with dressing.

> 1 serving equals: 1 lean meat exchange
> 1 vegetable exchange
> 80 calories

Chinese Chicken Salad (Makes 6 servings)

> **1 whole chicken breast**
> **2 cups chicken broth**
> **2 stalks celery**
> **6 green onions**
> **1/2 head of lettuce**

1. Cook chicken breast in broth until just done, about 20–25 minutes. Cool in broth.

2. Discard the skin. Pull the chicken meat from the bones in shreds.

3. Cut the celery and green onions into 2-inch lengths, then into sticks.

4. Shred the lettuce.

5. Mix all of the above together and keep in the refrigerator.

Dressing

>1/4 cup peanut oil
>1 Tbsp. sesame oil
>2 cloves garlic, finely chopped
>1 slice ginger, finely chopped
>2 Tbsp. soy sauce
>1/2 tsp. red pepper flakes (optional)

Mix all the ingredients together thoroughly and pour over salad just before serving.

>1 serving equals: 1 lean meat exchange
>2 fat exchanges
>145 calories

Crab Meat Stuffed Cucumber Salad (Makes 4 servings)

>1 large cucumber
>Small amount of salt
>1/4 lb. crab meat (canned or fresh cooked)
>2 egg yolks
>5 Tbsp. vinegar
>1/4 tsp. salt
>2 Tbsp. broth *dashi* #2 or water

1. Cut off both ends and peel the cucumber. Carefully scoop out the center. Put the remaining shell in salt water and let stand for 1 hour.
2. Mince the crab meat, removing all bones.
3. When the cucumber has softened, rinse it and wipe off any moisture.
4. Stuff the crab meat into the cucumber shell and chill in the refrigerator.
5. Make a sauce with the remaining ingredients. Put the egg yolks, broth, vinegar and salt into a pan and heat over a low heat. Stir constantly with a wooden spoon until liquid thickens. Remove from heat. Chill in refrigerator.
6. Cut the stuffed cucumber into 1/2-inch thick slices and arrange on serving dishes. Pour sauce over the top.

>1/4 of the cucumber slices equals: 1 lean meat exchange
>55 calories

Daikon Salad with Persimmon (Makes 6 servings)

>1 *daikon*, size of medium cucumber
>1/2 small cucumber, cubed
>1 persimmon, diced
>1 Tbsp. sugar

1/4 cup mild vinegar
Pinch of salt
1 Tbsp. freshly grated horseradish
1 Tbsp. freshly grated ginger root

1. Wash *daikon;* peel and grate fine.
2. Combine sugar, vinegar and salt and add to the *daikon.*
3. Mix the *daikon* with cucumber, persimmon, horseradish and ginger.
4. Serve equals portions on shredded lettuce.

1 serving equals: 1 fruit exchange
40 calories

Fruit Salad (Makes 6 servings)

1 cup pineapple chunks
1 orange, cut into hunks
1 small banana, sliced
5 dates, pitted, diced
1/4 cup chopped walnuts
Lettuce leaves
Dressing:
3 Tbsp. fresh lemon juice
3 Tbsp. coconut cream

1. Combine all the fruits and walnuts and toss gently. Set aside.
2. Combine lemon juice and coconut cream and mix thoroughly.
3. Arrange lettuce leaves on individual plates. Marinate each with the dressing.
4. Place equal amounts of the fruit mixture on each bed of lettuce.

1 serving equals: 1 fruit exchange
1 fat exchange
85 calories

Radish and Cucumber Salad (Makes 4 servings)

16 to 20 radishes
1 small cucumber
1 Tbsp. salt
4 Tbsp. vinegar
1/2 tsp. salt
2 Tbsp. soy sauce
1/4 tsp. vegetable oil

1. Cut the radishes into "roses." Remove the ends of the cucumber and

quarter it lengthwise. Scoop out the seeds and cut into slices 2-inches long and one-sixteenth-inch thick. Place the radishes and cucumbers in a shallow dish and sprinkle with 1 Tbsp. salt. Let stand 20 minutes. This will extract the excess liquid from the cucumber.

2. Rinse under cold running water and dry thoroughly.

3. Bring the vinegar to a boil in a small saucepan. Add salt and stir until dissolved. Cool the liquid; stir in the soy sauce and oil. Pour over radishes and cucumber; refrigerate for 30 minutes.

4. Pour off the liquid. Arrange the cucumber strips like a fan on the edge of the serving plate and place the radishes in the center.

1 serving equals: 1 vegetable exchange
25 calories

Watercress and Water Chestnut Salad (Makes 4 servings)

2 bunches watercress
9 peeled fresh water chestnuts or drained canned water chestnuts
1 tsp. soy sauce
2 tsp. vegetable oil
1/2 tsp. salt

1. With a small knife, trim and discard the tough ends of the watercress stems. Wash the watercress under cold running water, drop it into a pot of boiling water, then drain and pat the leaves dry with paper towels. With a cleaver or large knife, chop the watercress fine.

2. Wash and drain the water chestnuts; cut into 1/8-inch slices, then chop them fine.

3. Combine the soy sauce, vegetable oil, and salt in a large bowl; mix thoroughly.

4. Add the watercress and water chestnuts; toss them well with a large spoon so they are well coated with the mixture.

5. Chill and serve.

1 serving equals: 1 vegetable exchange
1/2 fat exchange
53 calories

Sauces and Dressings

Chive-Parsley Mayonnaise (Makes about 2 cups)

2 egg yolks
2 Tbsp. fresh lemon juice
2 Tbsp. white wine vinegar
1 tsp. salt
1 tsp. dry mustard
1/3 cups vegetable oil
1/3 cup finely chopped chives
3 Tbsp. minced fresh parsley

1. Combine egg yolks, lemon juice, vinegar, salt and mustard in blender; mix well.
2. With the machine running, slowly add oil in thin, steady stream and mix until thickened.
3. If too thick, add a little warm water.
4. Transfer to a bowl and stir in the chives and parsley.
5. Spoon into 2 sterilized half-pint jars and cover tightly.
6. Keep refrigerated.

1 Tbsp. equals: 2 fat exchanges
90 calories

Creamy Sprout Dressing (Makes 1 cup)

1-1/2 cups alfalfa sprouts
2 Tbsp. lemon juice or vinegar
1/2 cup vegetable oil
Salt and pepper to taste
1/2 tsp. mustard
2 tsp. chopped walnuts

1. Combine all ingredients in a blender or chop very fine, then pulverize with mortar and pestle.
2. Whirl smooth, about 1 minute.
3. Serve over green salad or use as a dip.

1 Tbsp. equals: 1-1/2 fat exchanges
65 calories

Herb Dressing ♯1 (Makes 3 cups)

> 1-1/3 cups white wine tarragon vinegar
> 1 cup vegetable oil
> 2/3 cup olive oil
> 3 tsp. mayonnaise
> 4 large garlic cloves, minced
> 2 tsp. Dijon mustard
> 1 tsp. salt
> 1 tsp. dried thyme
> 1/2 tsp. dried tarragon

1. Combine all ingredients in container with tight lid and shake well.
2. *Do not use blender;* garlic should remain minced.
3. Pour into bottles or other suitable containers with tight caps or corks. Try to distribute the garlic evenly among the containers.
4. Keep refrigerated. Shake well before using.

> 1 Tbsp. equals: 2 fat exchanges
>   90 calories

Herb Salad Dressing ♯2 (Makes 1-⅓ cups)

> 1 cup vegetable oil
> 1/3 cup lemon juice or white vinegar
> 1/2 tsp. salt
> 1/2 tsp. dry mustard
> 1/4 tsp. paprika
> 1/8 tsp. cayenne pepper
> 1/2 tsp. dried savory leaves
> 1/2 tsp. dried basil leaves
> 1/4 tsp. dried dill weed
> 1/2 clove garlic

1. Measure the oil and other ingredients into a jar. Cover.
2. Shake well. Chill. Remove the garlic before serving.

> 1 Tbsp. equals: 2 fat exchanges
>   90 calories

Lemon-Mustard Dressing (Makes 1 qt.)

> 3/4 cup dry white wine
> 2 Tbsp. dry mustard
> 8 egg yolks
> 2 cups vegetable oil

3 Tbsp. fresh lemon juice
1 Tbsp. chopped fresh chives or parsley
1 tsp. salt

1. Combine wine with mustard in large mixing bowl and let stand 1/2 hour.
2. Add egg yolks and mix well with whisk. Do not use electric mixer.
3. Add oil very slowly, beating constantly.
4. When dressing is thick, blend in all remaining ingredients.
5. Keeps well in refrigerator.

> 1 Tbsp. equals: 1-1/2 fat exchanges
> 65 calories

Parsley Sauce for Fish (Makes about 1 cup)

2 eggs
7 egg yolks
2 Tbsp. sugar
2 Tbsp. sake
1/4 tsp. salt
2 Tbsp. vinegar or lemon juice
1 cup minced parsley flakes

1. Mix the eggs and egg yolks in a pan and add the sugar, sake, salt, and vinegar in that order.
2. Heat the above mixture over low heat, stirring rapidly. Remove from heat, mix again, then put back on the heat while continuing to stir. A smooth sauce will develop.
3. Remove from the heat and stir until the sauce shines.
4. Mix the minced parsley with the egg sauce.

> 4 Tbsp. equal: 1 medium-fat meat exchange
> 1 fat exchange
> 1/2 fruit exchange or 1 vegetable
>   exchange
> 138 calories

Spicy Dipping Sauce for Fish (Makes ½ cup)

2 Tbsp. sake
1/4 cup grated *daikon*
2 scallion, including the trimmed green stem, sliced thin into rounds
1/4 cup all-purpose soy sauce

1/4 cup fresh lemon juice
1/8 tsp. seven-pepper spice

1.   Warm the sake in a small saucepan. Remove from heat, ignite it with a match and shake the pan gently until the flame goes out.
2.   Pour the sake into a small dish and cool.
3.   In a small mixing bowl, combine the sake and the grated *daikon*, sliced scallions, soy sauce, lemon juice and the seven-pepper spice.

This sauce may be used freely.

Sweet and Sour Sauce (Makes 1 cup)

1/4 cup brown sugar
1 Tbsp. cornstarch
1/4 cup cider vinegar
3/4 cup pineapple juice
1 Tbsp. soy sauce

1.   Combine all ingredients in a sauce pan.
2.   Cook over medium heat, stirring constantly until sauce thickens and becomes clear.

2 Tbsp. of sauce equals: 1 fruit exchange
40 calories

White Miso Dressing (Makes 1 qt.)

30 oz. packaged white soybean paste
1-1/4 cups sugar
1 cup sake
2 egg yolks

1.   Combine the soybean paste, sugar and sake in a 1-1/2-qt. saucepan and, stirring constantly, bring to a boil over moderate heat.
2.   Lower heat and simmer for 30 minutes, stirring from time to time to prevent the dressing from scorching.
3.   Remove pan from heat and beat in the egg yolks, 1 at a time.
4.   Place the pan in a large bowl of ice water to cool the dressing quickly.
5.   This may be used at once or stored in a tightly covered jar at room temperature for future use.

1 cup equals: 1 lean meat exchange and 9 bread
exchanges
1/3 cup equals: 3 bread exchanges

1/2 cup equals: 1/2 milk exchange and 4 bread
exchanges

1/4 cup equals: 1 vegetable exchange and 2 bread
exchanges

1 Tbsp. equals: 1/2 bread exchange and 34
calories

Turnip Relish (Makes 3 cups)

2 cups finely grated turnip
1 cup finely grated white onion
1/2 cup white wine vinegar
1/4 cup prepared horseradish
1 scant tsp. salt
Artificial sweetener equal to 3 Tbsp. sugar

1. Blend all ingredients in mixing bowl.
2. Spoon into sterilized jars and cover tightly.
3. Keep refrigerated.

1/4 cup equals: 1/2 vegetable exchange
14 calories

Spiced Malt Vinegar (Makes 1 qt.)

4 cups malt vinegar
8 whole cloves
4 bay leaves
2 tsp. pickling spice

1. Combine all ingredients in small saucepan.
2. Cover and simmer 20 to 25 minutes. Cool.
3. Pour into jars or tapered bottles and cover or cork.
4. Store in cool place at least 24 hours before using.
5. Strain before using.
6. This is very nice with any fried fish.

May be used freely.
No exchange necessary.

Vinaigrette Dressing (Makes ⅔ cups)

1 garlic clove, minced
1-1/2 tsp. salt
1 to 1-1/2 Tbsp. vinegar

1/2 tsp. Dijon mustard
1/8 tsp. freshly ground pepper
8 Tbsp. vegetable oil

1. Mince garlic by using garlic press or by pounding with tines of a fork. Transfer pulp to bowl.
2. Add all remaining ingredients except the oil and mix well.
3. Whisk in the oil with a fork, beating vigorously.
4. Let stand briefly before using.
5. Taste and adjust seasoning as desired.

1 Tbsp. equals: 2 fat exchanges
90 calories

Desserts

Caramel Fried Apples (Makes 16 wedges)

1/2 cup all-purpose flour, unsifted
2 Tbsp. cornstarch
3/4 tsp. baking powder
1/2 cup water
2 apples, 2-3/4-inch diameter, peeled, cored, and cut into 16 wedges
Vegetable oil
Caramel Coating:
2/3 cup granulated sugar
1/3 cup warm water
1 Tbsp. vegetable oil
2 tsp. sesame seeds

1. In a bowl, mix flour, cornstarch and baking powder. Add water and stir until smooth. Place fruit in batter and turn to coat.
2. In a deep pan, about 6 inches in diameter, pour oil to depth of 1-1/2 inches. Heat oil to 350°F. on a deep-frying thermometer. Using spoon, lift 1 piece of fruit at a time from batter, let excess batter drip off, then lower fruit into hot oil. Cook several pieces at a time until coating is a golden brown. Remove with a slotted spoon and drain on paper toweling.
3. Generously oil a flat serving dish. Fill a serving bowl to the brim with ice cubes; cover with water.
4. Place sugar, water and oil for the caramel coating in a 10-inch frying pan; stir to blend. Place pan over high heat. When mixture begins to bubble, shake pan continuously to prevent burning. Continue cooking and shaking pan until syrup just turns a pale straw color. Remove from heat, add sesame

seeds and swirl to mix.

5.   Drop fruit into syrup and swirl to coat evenly. Using 2 spoons, immediately remove each piece of fruit and place on oiled dish so pieces do not touch.

6.   Dip each piece of fruit in ice water so coating hardens and fruit cools.

1 wedge equals: 1-1/2 fruit exchanges
1/2 fat exchange
85 calories

Almond Cakes (Makes 36 cookies)

> **2-1/2 cups all-purpose flour**
> **3/4 cup sugar**
> **1/4 tsp. salt**
> **1 tsp. baking powder**
> **3/4 cup shortening**
> **1 egg plus the white of 1 egg to be brushed on the cookies**
> **2 Tbsp. water**
> **1-1/2 tsp. almond extract**
> **36 blanched whole almonds**

1.   Sift the flour, sugar, salt and baking powder into a large bowl.
2.   Blend shortening into the dry ingredients with a pastry fork.
3.   Beat the egg with water, add extract, then add to above mixture.
4.   Mix as you would for a pastry; when thoroughly blended, form into balls about the size of a walnut. Place on cookie sheet and press with the heel of your hand to flatten.
5.   Press 1 whole blanched almond on the top of each cookie and brush cookies with slightly beaten egg white.
6.   Bake in 350°F. oven for about 20–25 minutes.

1 cookie equals: 1 fruit exchange
1 fat exchange
85 calories

Almond Cream (Makes 16 squares)

> **1 qt. of whole milk**
> **1 qt. of half-and-half cream**
> **2 sticks agar-agar**
> **1-1/2 cups sugar**
> **7 tsp. almond extract**

1.   Pour milk and half-and-half cream into a large saucepan, more than a

3-qt. size.

2. Break the sticks of agar-agar into small pieces, drop into the pan and stir. Soak for 1 hour.

3. Cook mixture on medium heat for about 10 minutes to dissolve the agar-agar.

4. Add sugar and stir to dissolve.

5. Before adding the almond extract, be sure the agar-agar is entirely dissolved.

6. Strain through a sieve into a dry 9-inch cake pan. Allow to cool.

7. Refrigerate 2 hours to thicken. Serve when firm. Cut into 16 squares.

> 1 square equals: 1/2 cup whole milk and 1 bread exchange and 1 fat exchange
> or
> 1-1/2 bread exchanges and 2 fat exchanges
> 200 calories

Almond Float (Makes 10 servings)

> **2 envelopes unflavored gelatin**
> **1/2 cup cold water**
> **2 cups boiling water**
> **3/4 cup sugar**
> **1 Tbsp. almond extract**
> **1 cup milk**
> **2 cups mandarin oranges, water-packed, drained**

1. In a large bowl, sprinkle the gelatin over 1/2 cup cold water and let set to soften (about 5 minutes).

2. Add the boiling water, sugar, almond extract and milk.

3. Stir until sugar dissolves completely.

4. Pour mixture into a 9×9-inch square pan.

5. Refrigerate for 3 hours or until set firm.

6. Slice the almond float into small cubes and put into a serving bowl.

7. Top the float with mandarin sections.

> 1 serving equals: 2 fruit exchanges
> 80 calories

Lotus Seeds and Dates (Makes 6 servings)

> **7 oz. lotus seeds**
> **12 whole water chestnuts (canned)**
> **1/2 cup water**

8 oz. package pitted dates

1. Drain lotus seeds if canned. If dried seeds are used, cover with warm water and let stand for 30 minutes, drain, then simmer in water for 60 minutes. Rinse well under cold water, drain again.
2. Place lotus seeds and chestnuts in saucepan, add 1/2 cup water, simmer, stirring frequently, until the seeds are soft but not falling apart.
3. Add dates and simmer an additional 1 minute.
4. Remove from the heat and let cool, stirring occasionally.
5. Chill. You may add artificial sweetener to suit your taste.

> 1 serving equals: 1 bread exchange
> 2 fruit exchanges
> 148 calories

Strawberry Froth* (Makes 1 serving)

1 cup strawberries, fresh
1/2 egg white
1 tsp. plain gelatin

1. Mash strawberries.
2. Soften gelatin in cold water and dissolve over boiling water.
3. Mix with strawberries. Let mixture congeal (not too stiff).
4. Whip egg white and add to the mixture. Blend well.
5. Serve with a fresh strawberry on top.

> 1 serving equals: 1 fruit exchange
> 40 calories

---

* Courtesy of: Ulla S. Sahlen, Dietitian Nutrition Section, National Institute of Public Health, 104 01 Stockholm 60, Sweden.

Appendage

Sodium Restriction—Introduction

The hazards of high blood pressure are leading to an increased awareness of the amount of salt eaten. The old idea that an excess of salt may cause hypertension gains additional support almost daily. Salt, the condiment of the earth, is rapidly becoming the ingredient people are most concerned about in their diet. Many people lack genetic susceptibility and are immune to the effects of salt excesses; while others are susceptible. Ordinary table salt is sodium chloride. It is the sodium part of sodium chloride with which we are concerned. A constant ratio of sodium to water is maintained in all body fluids. Except under very unusual circumstances, this ratio never changes. The body cannot increase its amount of fluid without increasing its amount of sodium. If extra sodium is not available, no extra fluid can be retained. This is an oversimplification of human physiology, but it does explain why the low sodium diet is effective for conditions characterized by excessive fluid retention. Sometimes sodium restriction is used for high blood pressure; although there may be no fluid retention. In these cases, it is felt that lessening the sodium in the system helps to decrease the spasms of the blood vessels, thereby decreasing the elevation of blood pressure.

Blood pressure, unlike many medical terms, is self-explanatory. It is the pressure created against the walls of the arteries as blood flows through them. Blood pressure helps move the blood up to the brain and out to every part of the body.

Metabolic studies have shown that both children and adults require no more than 200 milligrams (mg.) of sodium per day—just about 1/10 of a teaspoon of table salt. The need increases for nursing women and for people working in hot, humid environments. Still, the intake of 200 mg. per day is adequate for the most strenuous circumstances.

The low-sodium or salt-free diet does not have to be bland or tasteless. However, saltless cooking is more complex than just leaving salt out of recipes. It means being able to become attuned to subtle flavors, using spices, herbs, and other flavorings instead of just seasoning with the sharpness of salt. Lemon or lime juice will awaken the flavors of food. Angostura bitters, usually associated with alcoholic beverages, will be very good on fish, chicken and vegetables.

Many low sodium food products are on the market. Available are low sodium canned vegetables, crackers, breads, cheeses, peanut butter, soups, tuna and salmon, as well as unsalted ham and bacon, low-sodium or milder soy sauce, salt-free butter and margarine and salad dressings. Cellu-Brand Commercial Sodium-Free baking powder is easily available. You can also use this "prescription" to be filled by a pharmacist:

Potassium bicarbonate	79.5 grams
Cornstarch	56.0 grams
Tartaric acid	15.0 grams
Potassium bitartarate	112.5 grams

Mix the powders thoroughly and sift several times before using. When using the sodium-free baking powder in baking, it should be added to the end of the mixing period and baked immediately.

Potassium bicarbonate can be used instead of baking soda in recipes. Because of after-taste, use half as much potassium bicarbonate as you would baking soda.

Salt substitutes vary in ingredients and are not universally recommended. There are many on the market. Neocurtasal, Featherweight "K" salt substitute, and Morton salt substitute are the most acceptable by patients according to taste tests. Morton's Light Salt contains equal parts of sodium chloride and potassium chloride. Individuals who must restrict their potassium intake should be aware of the contents of products being used. When the hypertensive patient receiving diuretic therapy requires potassium replacement, a salt substitute may be beneficial. It is conceivable that the use of a salt substitute containing large amounts of potassium by a person with renal (kidney) insufficiency, or of ammonium by those with severe liver disease may be ill advised. As a rule, mineral-based salt substitutes are not recommended for use in food processing. In addition to mineral-based salt substitutes, a number of so-called vegetized salts are also marketed. These range somewhere between condiments and salt substitutes. Most of these have powdered, dehydrated vegetables or vegetable powders as a base. Other ingredients may include yeast, bran, monosodium glutamate, lactates, malates, citrates, saccharated iron, magnesium carbonates, magnesium bromide, and a limited amount of sodium chloride, as well as sea salt. THE SPECIFIC DOSE OF A SALT SUBSTITUTE SHOULD BE CHECKED WITH A PHYSICIAN. If you do receive permission from your physician, it is wise to remember that salt substitutes tend to be bitter in large amounts.

A word should be said about licorice. There is a chemical present in it that causes the body to retain sodium, consequently raising the blood pressure. Most licorice made in the United States contains synthetic flavors, but that from England and Holland and perhaps other European countries is still made from the root of the glycyrrhiza (glis-i-rye-zuh) plant. This root is used as a flavoring and conditioning agent.

Water also deserves attention on the sodium restricted diet. Beware of a hidden source of sodium: your drinking water, especially if you own a water softening unit. You can easily check with your water department on the sodium content of the city water. Tap water should not exceed 20 mg. sodium per liter (1 liter equals 1.057 qts.). Attaching the water softener to the hot water only will provide the softness desired for washing without increasing the sodium content of the cold water used in cooking and drinking. Patients on very low sodium diets may have to use commercial bottled spring water, distilled water, or de-ionized water.

Foods that contain sodium do not always betray themselves by tasting salty. Some are sweet or have other flavors. The salt contained in processed foods and baked goods is invisible and beyond the individual's control. READ THE LABELS whenever possible.

The list of the most important sodium compounds added to foods is:

1. Salt (sodium chloride)—used in cooking or at the table, and also in processing.
2. Baking sodium (sodium bicarbonate)—used in leavened breads, and cakes; sometimes added to vegetables in cooking or used as an "alkalizer" for indigestion.
3. Brine (table salt and water)—used in processing foods to inhibit growth of bacteria, in cleaning or blanching vegetables and fruits, in freezing and canning certain foods and for flavor, as in corned beef, pickles, or sauerkraut.
4. Monosodium glutamate (sold under several brand names for home use)—used to enhance food flavor, especially in restaurant and hotel cooking, and in some packaged, canned and frozen foods.
5. Baking powder—used to leavened quick breads and cakes.
6. Di-sodium phosphate—present in some quick-cooking cereals and processed cheeses.
7. Sodium alginate—used in chocolate milks and ice creams for smooth texture.
8. Sodium benzoate—used as a preservative in condiments such as relishes, sauces, and salad dressings.
9. Sodium hydroxide—used in food processing to soften and loosen skin of ripe olives, hominy, certain fruits and vegetables. (It is used in preparing Dutch processed cocoa and chocolate, but the amount is not significant.)
10. Sodium propionate—used in pasturized cheeses and in some cakes to inhibit growth of mold.
11. Sodium sulfite—used to bleach certain fruits in which an artificial color is desired, such as maraschino cherries, glazed or crystallized fruit; used as a preservative in prunes or other dried fruits.

You need to be careful about only the first four sodium compounds in the above list—salt, baking soda, brine and monosodium glutamate. Try not to use monosodium glutamate when you cook, even though you may not always be able to avoid it in canned foods, or when you eat out.

In general, fruits contain very little natural sodium. Milk, meat, fish, poultry and eggs contain a relatively large amount of natural sodium. However, these are allowed because they are excellent sources of protein. Milk is our best source of calcium. Whether milk and its products are to be used will depend on how strict the sodium restriction is. Sometimes it is necessary to use a low-sodium milk preparation. These cases are very unusual. Vegetables range from those having very little natural sodium to those having quite a lot. Vegetables prepared in brine are high in sodium content. Avoid foods that are very salty.

In following the diet prescribed by your doctor, it is wise *to select the day's foods from this allowed list:*

—Fresh or frozen pork, beef, veal, lamb, liver, tongue, kidney, chicken, duck, squab, turkey or other fowls.

—Fresh or frozen fish (wash them thoroughly), oysters, clams, squid, scallops, sea cucumber, small amounts of shrimp and crab.

—Eggs, fresh.

—Soups, made without salt or monosodium glutamate (MSG).

—Beverages: tea, coffee, decaffeinated coffee, Ovaltine, milk.

—Dried legumes and nuts: tofu; green, red, soy, black beans; black-eyed peas and other beans; unsalted nuts; unsalted peanut butter.

—Starches: rice, noodles, rice noodles, rice vermicelli, hot cereal, dry cereals limited to puffed rice, puffed wheat and shredded wheat; water chestnut flour, cornstarch, wheat flour, plain sheet rice noodles, sweet dumplings, sweet bou.

—Vegetables: all fresh and frozen vegetables and melons.

—Fruits: all fresh and frozen and canned fruits (without sugar if on a sugar restriction) and juices.

—Breads and crackers, desserts: small amount of bread, cakes, cookies, pies, puddings, candies, dim sum. Some of these items may be allowed in your diet and some may not. Consult your nutrition counselor.

—Fats and oils: corn, soy, cottonseed, peanut, safflower, sesame oils; lard and vegetable shortenings, unsalted sweet butter or unsalted margarine; sometimes salted butter and salted margarine will be allowed in small amounts (2 teaspoons per day).

—Condiments and seasonings: see page 135.

The high-sodium foods which should be avoided or restricted are:

—Processed foods: certain cheeses, instant and most ready-to-eat cereals, instant noodles.

—Canned and instant soups and bouillon cubes, meat extracts.

—Catsup, chili sauce, prepared mustard, prepared horseradish, barbecue sauce, soy and Worcestershire sauce, oyster sauce, hoisin sauce, fermented black bean sauce, dried black bean sauce, any salted beans, Chinese barbecue sauce, fermented bean curd, seafood sauce, hot bean paste, shrimp paste, pickled soy bean curd, celery salt, onion salt, sea salt, garlic salt, seaweed, yellow bean paste, chili paste, preserved tofu, roux paste (dried curry leaves); sweet miso, salty light miso, salty dark miso, powdered *mame*-miso.

—Pickles, relishes, olives, sauerkraut, and other foods prepared in brine and salt water; pickled green vegetables and root vegetables; meat tenderizers, monosodium glutamate (MSG).

—Regular canned vegetables and some frozen vegetables (peas, corn, lima beans); salted, pickled or dried vegetables, soy preserved cucumbers, regular canned tomato juice and V-8 juice.

—Fruits: any salted fruits.

—Salty or smoked meats: bologna, corned or chipped beef, Frankfurters, ham, bacon, luncheon meats, canned meats, salt pork, sausages, smoked tongue, barbecued meats; Chinese sausages, Chinese ham, cured gizzards; brains, kidneys and liver are also high in sodium but will sometimes be allowed in small amounts.

—Salted or smoked or canned fish: anchovies, caviar, salted or dried cod, herring, sardines, dried cuttle fish, shrimp, smoked salmon, lox, most canned fish, shellfish (dried and salted), *kamaboko* (fish cake).

—Salted and preserved eggs, chemical eggs.

—Snack items: potato chips, french fries, pretzels, salted popcorn, salted nuts, salted crackers, shrimp chips.

—Bacon fat; large amounts of regular butter or margarine and the commercial salad dressings.

—Meat analogs (vegetable proteins modified to simulate the texture and flavor of various meats, poultry, and seafoods).

Spices and Herbs

Spices and herbs include a great variety of vegetable products which are aromatic and pungent. Spices are certain parts of plants such as dried seeds, buds, fruit, flowers, bark or roots. Herbs are from the leafy parts. Spices are sold in whole or ground form. They gradually lose flavor and color during storage and should not be purchased in quantity. They should be stored in a cool, dry place in air-tight containers. The flavor of ground spices is imparted immediately, so they may be added about 15 minutes before the end of the cooking period. Whole spices are best in slow-cooking dishes, such as braised meats or stews; they are added at the beginning of the cooking period so that the long simmering can extract the full flavor and aroma. To release their flavor, whole or leaf herbs should be crumbled finely just before they are to be used. Whole spices should be tied in a cheesecloth bag for easy removal. Flavoring seeds, such as sesame seeds, may be toasted before using to enhance their flavor.

Specific herbs and spices will complement certain foods. The following list is a guide to put delicious enjoyment back into meals where sodium has been reduced.

Beef:	Allspice, anise, basil, bay leaf, caraway seed, cayenne, pepper, celery seed, Chinese vinegar, cloves, coriander, cumin, curry powder, dill, fennel, Five Spice Powder, garlic, ginger, lemon, lime, mace, marigold, marjoram, mint, mustard (dry), onion powder, oregano, paprika, pepper, rosemary, sage, savories, tarragon, thyme.
Pork:	Anise, basil, *bergamot*, caraway seed, *chervil*, cinnamon, cloves, coriander, cumin, curry powder, dill, fennel, ginger, hot red pepper, lemon, lemon balm, mint, marjoram, onion powder, oregano, paprika, parsley, pepper, rosemary, sage, savories, tarragon, thyme.
Veal:	Basil, curry powder, ginger, lemon, lemon balm, lime, marjoram, onion powder, paprika, parsley, poultry seasoning, pepper, rosemary, sage, tarragon, thyme.
Lamb:	Basil, bay leaves, caraway seed, coriander, cinnamon, cumin, curry powder, dill, ginger, lemon balm, hyssop, marjoram, mint, oregano, paprika, parsley, rosemary, sage, savories, tarragon, thyme.
Poultry:	Angostura bitters, basil, bay leaf, caraway seed, cayenne pepper, celery seed, cinnamon, coriander, cumin, curry powder, dill, Five Spice Powder, garlic, ginger, lemon, lemon balm, mace, marigold, marjoram, mint, nutmeg, oregano, paprika, parsley, pepper, poultry seasoning, rosemary, saffron, sage, savories, tarragon, thyme.
Fish and Seafood:	Allspice, anise, angostura bitters, basil, bay leaf, caraway, chives, cinnamon, cloves, coriander, curry, dill, fennel, Five Spice Powder, garlic, ginger, hyssop, lemon, lemon balm, lime, mace, marigold, marjoram, mint, nutmeg, oregano, paprika, parsley, pepper, rosemary, saffron, sage, savories, tarragon, thyme, tumeric.
Liver:	Coriander, Five Spice Powder, sage, tarragon.
Eggs:	Allspice, anise, basil, bay leaf, cayenne pepper, celery seed, chervil, chili powder, chives, cumin, curry powder, dill, fennel, lemon balm, lovage, marjoram, mint, mustard (dry), nutmeg, onion powder, oregano, paprika, parsley, poppy seed, rosemary, sage, savories, tarragon, thyme, tumeric.
Cheese:	Allspice, anise, basil, caraway, cayenne pepper, celery seed, chili powder, dill, fennel, oregano, paprika, parsley, pepper (red), poppy seed, saffron, sage, thyme.
Rice:	Basil, caraway, curry, saffron, tumeric.
Curried Dishes:	Curry, pepper (red), saffron.
Fruits:	Allspice, anise seed, cardamon, celery seed, cinnamon,

cloves, curry powder, Five Spice Powder, ginger, mace, nutmeg, poppy seed, rosemary.

Vegetables: Allspice, angostura bitters, basil, caraway, cardamon, cayenne pepper, celery seeds, cinnamon, cloves, curry powder, dill, fennel, ginger, lemon, lime, mace, marjoram, mint, mustard (dry), mustard seed, nutmeg, onion powder, oregano, paprika, poppy seed, pepper, rosemary, sage, savories, sesame seed, tarragon, thyme.

Salads: Allspice, anise, basil, bay leaf, bergamot, borage, caraway, catmint, celery seed, chervil, chickweed, Chinese vinegar, chives, cloves, comfrey, coriander, cumin, curry powder, dandelion, dill, elder, garlic, hyssop, lemon, lemon balm, marigold, mint, mustard seed, oregano, paprika, parsley, poppy seed, roses, salad burnet, savories, sesame seed, sweet cicely, tarragon, thyme.

Soups: Anise, basil, bay leaf, borage, caraway, cardamon, celery seed, chives, cinnamon, cloves, cumin, curry powder, dill, fennel, garlic, hyssop, lemon balm, lovage, mace, marigold, marjoram, mint, onion powder, oregano, paprika, parsley, pepper, poultry seasoning, rosemary, saffron, sage, savories, sesame seed, stinging nettle, tarragon, thyme.

Baked Products and Breads: Allspice, anise seed, basil, caraway, celery seed, cinnamon, cloves, coriander, cumin, curry powder, dill, fennel, garlic, ginger, lovage, mace, marigold, marjoram, onion powder, parsley, poppy seed, rosemary, saffron, sesame seed, tumeric.

Other allowed condiments, spices and herbs are:

Green onion, dried mushroom, golden needle, wood ear, red dates, sweet dates, dried lily flower, dried orange peel, hot pepper sauce (Tabasco), dried fungus, Fragrant Green, Star Anise, sugar, honey, jam (if allowed in the diet by the nutrition counselor and physician), *kin chow*, wine, sherry, *togarashi* (pepper, orange peel, sesame seeds), *sansho* or *fah chui* (from berries or leaves of the zanthoxylum plant (sometimes referred to as the Chinese wing leaf), prickly ash, Chinese pepper seeds, *shiso* or *jel shoh* (comes from the perilla plant that produces the pepper leaf and may be used fresh, dried or powdered), star fruit (can substitute for the lemon), tamarind (can substitute for lemon juice or vinegar), *laos* or *lingkuas* (ginger-like root).

Sauces which may be used very sparingly when diluted with water for marinades for meats are:

Hoisin, which is sweet and strong with garlic and fruit flavor.

Chee Hou, which is sweet with celery and black pepper flavor.

Chap Sam, which is sweet with hot chili peppers and fruit flavor.

Frequently allowed for cooking in very limited amounts are milder soy sauce and table salt. These are not to be used at the same time. A scant 1/2 teaspoon of table salt or 5 teaspoons of the milder soy sauce (Kikkoman) are about equal in sodium content.

Sodium is measured by weight in units called milligrams (mg.). An example would be 1 level teaspoon of table salt (5 grams) contains about 2300 milligrams of sodium. One level teaspoon of milder soy sauce (Kikkoman) contains 202 milligrams of sodium (202 mg.).

Emphasis must be place on the *importance of always checking* with your doctor before using *any medicine* he has not prescribed. There are some medicines that may contain sodium: "alkalizers" for indigestion, headache remedies (other than plain aspirin), cough medicines, laxatives, antibiotics and sedatives. Do not use baking soda as a medicine.

The following recipes in this book have been calculated to indicate the total milligrams of sodium per serving. The milligrams are indicated in the abbreviated form of "mg." Also given is the total calories per serving and the number of food exchanges for each recipe.

Recipes with Sodium Restriction

Soups

Spinach and Bean Curd Soup (Makes 4 servings)

> 8 oz. bean curd
> 4 cups vegetable stock, unsalted
> 2 cups diagonally cut fresh spinach
> 1/4 tsp. white pepper
> 1 tsp. minced ginger
> Vermicelli, a few strands
> 1/2 tsp. sesame oil
> 1 Tbsp. dry sherry
> 1 tsp. milder soy sauce (Kikkoman)
> 4 tsp. chopped scallion

1.   Place refrigerated bean curd under a weight in an absorbent towel until it is similar to Farmers' cheese in consistency. This will take several hours or overnight. Cut into 1/2-inch cubes and set aside.

2.   Bring stock to a boil and simmer greens gently until they are barely

tender. Season with pepper and ginger. Add several strands of vermicelli (rice stick). Gently slide bean curd into soup and simmer a couple minutes longer.

3. Add sesame oil, sherry and soy sauce.
4. Flavor with chopped scallion just before serving.

> 1 serving equals: 1/2 lean meat exchange
> 1 vegetable exchange
> 70 mg. sodium
> 53 calories

Chicken

Lemon Chicken (Makes 4 servings)

> 4 unskinned chicken breast halves, boned, flattened to 1/2-inch thickness
> 3 Tbsp. vegetable oil
> 2/3 cup each of bean sprouts, thinly sliced snow peas, thinly sliced bamboo
>   shoots
> 1/2 cup of thinly sliced water chestnuts
> Marinade:
>   1 Tbsp. vegetable oil
>   1 tsp. milder soy sauce (Kikkoman)
>   1/2 tsp. sherry
>   Dash of freshly ground pepper
> Lemon Sauce:
>   3/4 cup water
>   1 tsp. sugar or fructose*
>   Juice of 1 lemon
>   1 tsp. vegetable oil
>   1 tsp. cornstarch dissolved in small amount of water
> Garnish:
>   tomato wedges, lemon slices and green onion slices

1. For the marinade, combine the first 4 ingredients in a small bowl. Rub over chicken, allowing excess to drain off. Coat lightly with cornstarch.
2. Refrigerate for 30 minutes.
3. For the lemon sauce, combine the first 5 ingredients in a small saucepan, bring to boil over medium-high heat, stirring constantly. Add dissolved cornstarch and stir until slightly thickened. Keep warm.
4. Heat vegetable oil in large skillet over medium-high heat until a light haze forms. Fry chicken until golden brown on each side. Drain, cut into

---

* If artificial sweetener is used, it should be added *after* the cooking and used in the amount that is equal to 1 tsp. of sugar or fructose. Use the sugar or fructose only with the permission of your physican or nutrition counselor.

strips 3/4-inch wide. Set aside and keep warm.

5. Wipe out skillet, add small amount of vegetable oil and heat over medium-high heat. Add sprouts, snow peas, bamboo shoots and chestnuts, and stir-fry until crisp tender.

6. Garnish with tomato wedges, lemon slices and green onion slices.

> 1 serving equals: 3 lean meat exchanges
> 1 vegetable exchange
> 70 mg. sodium
> 190 calories

Classic Chicken with Peaches (Makes 6 servings)

16 oz. can cling peach slices (canned without sugar)
2 Tbsp. vegetable oil
6 chicken breast halves, boned, skinned
1 clove garlic, crushed
1/2 cup white wine
1/2 cup chicken broth, unsalted
1/4 tsp. marjoram
1/2 cup half-and-half
2 egg yolks, beaten
Pepper to taste

1. Drain peaches, set aside.
2. Heat oil in large skillet over medium-high heat.
3. Cook chicken breasts until lightly browned.
4. Add garlic, wine, chicken broth and marjoram.
5. Bring to boil, stirring to prevent sticking. Reduce heat, cover and simmer over medium-low heat for 10 minutes.
6. Remove chicken from sauce.
7. Bring sauce to boil, stirring constantly. Remove from heat.
8. Mix the half-and-half with the beaten egg yolk. Stir a little of the broth sauce into the beaten egg mixture, then stir the egg yolk mixture into the sauce. Stir continuously until mixture thickens.
9. Return chicken to pan along with peach slices. Cover and simmer 2 minutes or until chicken is heated through. Season with pepper to taste.

> 1 serving equals: 4 lean meat exchanges
> 1 fruit exchange
> 73 mg. sodium
> 260 calories

Chicken with Plum Sauce (Makes 6 servings)

> 3 chicken breasts, skinned and boned
> 1 Tbsp. lemon juice
> 1 Tbsp. cornstarch dissolved in 1 Tbsp. water
> 1/4 tsp. sesame oil
> Dash of white pepper
> 2 Tbsp. vegetable oil
> Batter:
> 3/4 cup all-purpose flour
> 1/4 cup cornstarch
> 1-1/2 tsp low sodium baking powder
> 1 cup water
> 3 Tbsp. vegetable oil

1. Cut chicken into pieces about 2-inches square. Pound chicken lightly with back of cleaver or heavy knife so each piece is uniform in thickness.

2. In a bowl, combine juice, water, cornstarch, sesame oil and pepper. Add chicken and stir to coat, then stir in 1 Tbsp. of vegetable oil and let stand for 15–20 minutes to marinate.

3. In another bowl, combine the flour, cornstarch and baking powder. Add remaining 1 Tbsp. of vegetable oil and water, and blend until smooth. Let the batter rest for 10 minutes.

4. In a wide frying pan, pour vegetable oil for frying the meat. Dip each piece of chicken in batter, then place in hot oil. Fry chicken without crowding, turning occasionally, until crust is golden brown and the meat is no longer pink.

5. Remove with a slotted spoon and drain on paper towels.

6. Keep warm in 200°F. oven until all pieces are cooked.

7. Serve with plum sauce. See recipe below.

1 serving of chicken equals: 3 lean meat exchanges
1 bread exchange
1 fat exchange
10 mg. sodium
278 calories

Plum Sauce (Makes 1 cup)

> 3/4 cup water
> 1-1/2 tsp. cornstarch.
> Artificial sweetener to equal 2 tsp. sugar
> 1 tsp. milder soy sauce (Kikkoman)
> 3 plums, pitted, fresh or canned without sugar
> 1 Tbsp. vegetable oil
> 1 tsp. fresh, thinly sliced ginger root

1. In a small pan, heat 1 Tbsp. vegetable oil over medium-high heat.
2. Add the sliced ginger root and stir-fry for 30 seconds.
3. Mix water, cornstarch, soy sauce with canned or fresh plums.
4. Pour plum sauce mixture onto the ginger root and cook, stirring, until sauce bubbles and thickens slightly. Remove from heat and add the artificial sweetener.

1 Tbsp. equals: no exchange necessary
13 mg. sodium
7 calories

1/4 cup equals: 1 vegetable exchange or 1/2 fruit exchange
50 mg. sodium
27 calories

Spiced Chicken (Makes 6 servings)

1/4 cup all-purpose flour
1/8 tsp. cayenne pepper
1/8 tsp. nutmeg
2-1/2 lbs. broiler-fryer chicken, cut in parts
3 Tbsp. vegetable oil
1 tsp. dried thyme
1 tsp. tarragon leaves
1/2 cup dry white wine
4 lemon wedges

1. In small bowl stir together flour, cayenne pepper, nutmeg. Coat chicken on all sides.
2. In large skillet or wok heat the oil over medium-high heat.
3. Add chicken and brown well on all sides.
4. Sprinkle with thyme and tarragon leaves.
5. Pour wine over chicken. Cover.
6. Reduce heat and cook 40 minutes or until chicken is fork-tender.
7. Serve with lemon wedges to be squeezed over each serving.

1 serving equals: 3 lean meat exchanges
56 mg. sodium
185 calories
Bread exchange negligible

Chicken with Vegetables and Enokidake Mushrooms (Makes 4 servings)

1/2 cup *enokidake* mushrooms, cut off ends and rinse
2 garden onions, minced

1/4 cup celery, diced
2 tsp. vegetable oil
1/4 cup minced green bell pepper
1/4 cup shredded *daikon*
1 cup cooked chicken, cubed
1 Tbsp. canned pimento, cut in strips
2 Tbsp. cornstarch
1 cup chicken broth, unsalted
1/4 tsp. tarragon, crushed
Dash of garlic powder
Black pepper to taste
1 tsp. milder soy sauce (Kikkoman)
2 tsp. lemon juice

1.   Add 1 tsp. vegetable oil to skillet. Add mushrooms, onion, celery and stir-fry for 2 minutes. Set aside in dish.

2.   Add 1 tsp. vegetable oil to skillet and stir-fry minced green pepper for 4 minutes. Set aside with the mushrooms and onions, etc.

3.   Dissolve cornstarch in small amount of cold chicken broth. Add this to the remaining broth. Add tarragon, garlic powder, pepper, soy sauce and lemon juice. Place over medium heat, stirring constantly, and cook until sauce begins to thicken.

4.   Add the chicken pieces. Cook to the desired thickness of sauce or until the chicken is thoroughly heated. Add pimento.

5.   Serve with rice. Half-cup of cooked rice equals 1 bread exchange.

1 serving equals: 1 lean meat exchange
1/2 fat exchange
1 vegetable exchange
79 mg. sodium
138 calories

Green Peppers Stuffed with Chicken (Makes 6 servings)

2 Tbsp. vegetable oil
12 oz. chicken meat, boned, skinned, diced
1 large onion, peeled and diced
2 cups tomatoes, fresh, peeled, cut into wedges
1/4 tsp. pepper
1/2 tsp. marjoram, crushed
4 slices soft bread, low sodium, crumbled
3 green peppers
Paprika for garnish

1.   Stir-fry meat and onion in cooking oil over medium heat for 5 minutes.

2.   Add tomatoes, pepper and marjoram. Simmer for 10 minutes.

3. Add bread crumbs to the meat and vegetable mixture. Toss gently. Set aside.

4. Cut peppers in half, remove seeds and stems and cook in boiling water for 3 minutes. Drain thoroughly.

5. Fill pepper halves with mixture. Sprinkle paprika on top.

6. Arrange on greased baking dish. Bake in 350°F. oven for 30 minutes.

> 1 serving equals: 1 bread exchange
> 2 lean meat exchanges
> 60 mg. sodium
> 123 calories

Veal

Veal Paprika (Makes 4 servings)

> **3 Tbsp. vegetable oil**
> **1 lb. veal chuck, cut into 1-inch cubes**
> **6 small onions or scallions, quartered**
> **1 clove garlic, minced or pressed**
> **2 Tbsp. tomato paste, unsalted**
> **1 cup water**
> **1/2 cup dry red wine**
> **1 tsp. paprika**
> **Dash of pepper**
> **1/4 lb. fresh mushrooms, sliced**

1. In a large skillet or wok heat the oil over medium-high heat.

2. Brown the veal on all sides, remove from skillet.

3. Add onions and garlic, cook, stirring constantly, 2 minutes. Stir in tomato paste, loosening brown bits from the bottom of pan.

4. Add veal, water, wine, paprika and pepper; cover.

5. Stirring occasionally, cook 30 minutes or until veal is almost tender.

6. Add mushrooms; cook 15 minutes longer or until veal is tender.

> 1 serving equals: 2 lean meat exchanges
> 1 vegetable exchange
> 2 fat exchanges
> 70 mg. sodium
> 225 calories

Pork

Low Sodium Pork Sausage (Makes 14 patties)

>2 lbs. lean pork, all visible fat removed, ground twice
>1 Tbsp. dried sage, crushed
>1 tsp. garlic powder
>1 tsp. onion powder
>1 tsp. ground mace
>1 tsp. ground black pepper
>1/4 tsp. ground allspice
>1/4 tsp. ground cloves
>1/4 tsp. oregano, crushed

1. Combine all ingredients in large mixing bowl and mix thoroughly.
2. Form into 14 patties.

>1 patty equals: 1 high-fat meat exchange
>1 fat exchange
>39 mg. sodium
>142 calories

Pork with Vegetables (Makes 4 servings)

>1/2 lb. lean pork (butt or pork shoulder)
>1 Tbsp. vegetable oil
>1 Tbsp. fermented black beans, rinsed, drained
>1 tsp. finely minced fresh ginger root
>1/2 Tbsp. minced garlic
>1 cup cabbage or Chinese celery cabbage, cut into 1-inch strips
>1/2 cup green bell pepper, cut into 1-inch pieces
>1/2 cup chicken broth, unsalted
>1/2 tsp. chopped fresh hot red pepper
>2 scallions, cut into 1-inch pieces
>1 tsp. cornstarch blended with 1 tsp. cold water to dissolve
>1 tsp. vegetable oil

1. Place pork in pot and add water to cover. Allow water to come to a full boil, reduce heat and simmer 45 minutes or until the meat is done.
2. Remove pork from the water and slice it across the grain into 1/4-inch slices.
3. Heat wok or skillet over high heat 1 minute; add vegetable oil and heat until the oil smokes.
4. Add black beans, pork, ginger, and garlic; mash them together a half-minute to create a strong smell, do not let them burn in the hot oil.

5. Add cabbage and green pepper and stir over high-heat 1 minute.

6. Add chicken broth, red pepper and stir until blended. Add scallions and liquid cornstarch.

> 1 serving equals: 1 high-fat meat exchange
> 2 fat exchanges
> 62 mg. sodium
> 185 calories

Fried Pork with Vegetables and Noodles (Makes 4 servings)

2 Tbsp. scallions, chopped
2 Tbsp. ground sesame seeds
1 tsp. milder soy sauce (Kikkoman)
2 Tbsp. rice wine
1 lb. very lean pork cut into small pieces
1 Tbsp. vegetable oil
1 green pepper, seeded, minced
1 cucumber, sliced into thin strips
1 tomato, sliced into thin strips
2 oz. transparent noodles or very thin spaghetti
Sauce:
2 Tbsp. vinegar
1 tsp. freshly ground black pepper
Artificial sweetener to equal 1 Tbsp. sugar

1. Mix scallions, sesame seeds, soy sauce, and wine. Marinate pork in this mixture for 1 hour.

2. Heat oil in skillet or wok over medium heat. Drain pork; brown well on both sides in hot oil.

3. Prepare noodles or spaghetti by cooking in boiling unsalted water until tender. Rinse in cold water and drain. Hold over heat or warm up.

4. Combine noodles with cucumber and tomato strips. Place on one side of serving platter.

5. Place pork on other side of platter.

6. Blend ingredients for the sauce and pour over the pork.

> 1 serving equals: 2 medium-fat meat exchanges
> 1 vegetable exchange
> 1/2 cup noodles: 1 bread exchange
> 73 mg. sodium
> 239 calories

Barbecued Spareribs (Makes 4 servings)

2 lbs. very lean spareribs, fresh

1 tsp. milder soy sauce (Kikkoman)
1 Tbsp. orange honey
1 clove garlic, chopped
1/2 tsp. hot chili oil
1 green onion, chopped
1 Tbsp. rice wine or sherry

1. Mix all ingredients.
2. Chop ribs into 2-inch sections; marinate in liquid mixture for 4 to 6 hours, turning several times. This can be marinated overnight; keep refrigerated; allow to warm up before baking.
3. Preheat oven to 350°F.
4. Drain the ribs; retain liquid.
5. Place ribs on rack in a roasting pan. Bake 325°F. for 45 minutes, basting with the marinade every 15 minutes.
6. Turn up heat to 375°F. and finish baking undisturbed 15 minutes until slightly crusty.
7. Serve hot.

1 serving equals: 3 high-fat meat exchanges
3 fat exchanges
1/2 fruit exchange
83 mg. sodium
440 calories

Sweet and Sour Pork (Makes 6 servings)

1-1/2 lbs. boneless very lean pork butt, cut in 1-inch cubes
1/2 tsp. Five Spices seasoning
2 Tbsp. *hoisin* sauce
1 Tbsp. rice wine or dry sherry
1 Tbsp. toasted sesame seeds

1. Combine meat with Five Spices seasoning, *hoisin* sauce, and wine; marinate 2 to 4 hours.
2. Bake in 400°F. oven for 40 minutes. Drain off any fat and add pork to the sweet and sour fruit sauce. Reheat and sprinkle with sesame seeds.

Sweet and Sour Fruit Sauce

1 cup pineapple chunks, canned without sugar
15 lichees, canned without sugar
1/4 cup rice wine vinegar
1 Tbsp. low sodium tomato catsup
1 Tbsp. cornstarch
1 bell pepper, seeded and cut up into chunks
1/2 onion, cut into slender slices

Artificial sweetener equal to 2 Tbsp. sugar

1. Drain fruits and measure liquid to make 1 cup, adding water if necessary.

2. Set fruits aside and combine juice with vinegar, catsup and cornstarch. Cook and stir over medium heat until thickened and clear.

3. Add fruits, green pepper, onion and bring to boil. Add artificial sweetener after removing from the heat.

> 1 serving equals: 3 high-fat meat exchanges
> 1 fruit exchange
> 1 fat exchange
> 46 mg. sodium
> 275 calories

Fish and Seafood

Fish Omelet (Makes 1 serving)

> 1 egg, well beaten
> 1/2 tsp. vegetable oil
> 1/4 cup tuna, unsalted, water-packed (dietetic) or fresh, cooked in unsalted water
> 2 tsp. pimiento, cut into small pieces
> 1/2 cup peas, fresh or canned without salt
> 1/2 tsp. rosemary seasoning, crushed

1. To the beaten egg, add fish, pimiento, peas and rosemary. If the peas are fresh, cook them first in unsalted water.

2. Add vegetable oil to frying pan and place over medium heat.

3. Add egg mixture. Lift edges of omelet as it cooks. Tip frying pan to allow liquid to run under the firm portion.

4. Slip omelet onto a plate then return it to the pan upside-down. Brown that side also.

> 1 serving equals: 2 medium-fat meat exchanges
> 1 vegetable exchange
> 84 mg. sodium
> 135 calories

Steamed Fish (Makes 6 servings)

> 1-1/2 lbs. white fish, raw, cleaned
> 3 Tbsp. lemon juice
> 1 tsp. ginger root, finely chopped

1 Tbsp. vegetable oil
2 Tbsp. finely chopped green onion

1. Place fish on a plate, then place on rack above boiling water.
2. Steam in high heat for about 20 minutes or until the fish is firm.
3. Drain off the juice.
4. Put the other ingredients on top of fish, and serve.

1 serving equals: 2 lean meat exchanges
51 mg. sodium
110 calories

Crab in Black Bean Sauce (Makes 6 servings)

2 cups flaked crab meat, fresh, steamed in water
1 Tbsp. vegetable oil
1 Tbsp. fermented black beans, rinsed, drained and finely chopped
1 small clove garlic, minced
1/4 tsp. minced fresh ginger root
1 small green pepper, seeded and cut into 1-inch squares
1 Tbsp. dry sherry
2 whole green onions, cut into 1-inch lengths
1/3 cup chicken broth, unsalted

1. Heat wok or skillet over high heat. When pan is hot, add oil. When the oil begins to heat, add black beans, garlic and ginger. Stir-fry for 5–10 seconds.
2. Add green pepper and stir-fry for 1 minute.
3. Add crab, sherry, onion and chicken broth.
4. Cook, stirring until crab is hot.

1 serving equals: 2 lean meat exchanges
124 mg. sodium
110 calories

Bean Curd

Spiced Soybean Curd (Makes 5 servings)

4 pieces of soybean curd (1 piece is 2-1/2 × 2-3/4 × 1 inch)
2 oz. fresh lean pork, minced
1 Tbsp. vegetable oil
1 tsp. chopped garlic
1 Tbsp. chili oil
1-1/2 tsp. milder soy sauce (Kikkoman)

1 tsp. pepper
1/2 cup water
1/4 tsp. cornstarch
1 Tbsp. chopped green onion
1/8 tsp. sesame oil

1.   Cut the soybean curd into 1/2-inch cubes. Place in boiling water for a minute, then drain.

2.   Heat the oil in skillet or wok over medium-high heat.

3.   Add minced pork, garlic, chili oil, soy sauce and pepper. Stir-fry to mix.

4.   Add soybean curd, water and cornstarch. Cook over low heat for a few minutes.

5.   Add chopped green onion and sesame oil. Serve.

> 1 serving equals: 1 lean meat exchange
> 1 fat exchange
> 63 mg. sodium
> 130 calories

Bean Curd in Barbecue Sauce (Makes 4 servings)

8 oz. bean curd
2 cups fresh peas
3 Tbsp. peanut oil
3 cloves minced garlic
1 tsp. minced fresh ginger
2 tsp. milder soy sauce (Kikkoman)
2 Tbsp. dry sherry
1 tsp. Five Spices seasoning
Few drops sesame oil
1 cup scallions, diagonally cut
Fresh cilantro (coriander) leaves for garnish

1.   Place refrigerated bean curd under weight in an absorbent towel until it is similar to Farmers' cheese in consistency. This will take several hours or overnight. Cut into 1/4 × 2 × 2-inch pieces. Set aside.

2.   Blanch peas in 1/2 cup water 4 minutes or until tender. Do not over-cook. Drain, cover and set aside. Retain liquid.

3.   In wok or skillet, heat peanut oil to smoking. Gently fry bean curd pieces until golden brown. Avoid excessive stirring.

4.   Combine garlic, ginger, soy sauce, sherry, honey, Five Spices seasoning and sesame oil. Add this sauce directly to wok. Simmer 2 to 3 minutes, making sure all pieces of bean curd are covered with sauce in order that they may absorb flavor and color.

5.   Add cooked peas, their liquid and 1 cup cut fresh scallions. Stir-fry for

a minute to heat through. Serve on a platter garnished with fresh cilantro leaves.

> 1 serving equals: 1 lean meat exchange
> 1-1/2 bread exchanges
> 2 fat exchanges
> 105 mg. sodium
> 247 calories

Bean Curd with Walnuts and Broccoli (Makes 4 servings)

8 oz. bean curd
3 cups fresh broccoli pieces
1 cup walnuts, chopped
2 Tbsp. cornstarch
2 tsp. Five Spices seasoning
2 Tbsp. water or vegetable stock
2 Tbsp. dry sherry
2 tsp. milder soy sauce (Kikkoman)
1 tsp. cornstarch
1/2 tsp. sesame oil
2 Tbsp. peanut oil
1 clove garlic, minced
1 tsp. minced ginger

1.   Place refrigerated bean curd under weight in an absorbent towel until it is similar to Farmers' cheese in consistency. This will take several hours or overnight.
2.   Cut flowerettes, leaves and tender stalks of broccoli into pieces, using diagonal cuts. Set aside.
3.   Make a sauce by combining water or stock, sherry, soy sauce, cornstarch and sesame oil.
4.   Cut bean curd into $1/2 \times 2 \times 2$-inch pieces; dust lightly with a mixture of the cornstarch and Five Spices seasoning; keep separated on a paper. Gently fry bean curd pieces until they are golden brown. Avoid excessive stirring. Remove from wok and set aside.
5.   Heat peanut oil in wok until very hot. Working quickly, fry garlic and ginger until golden. Stir in broccoli pieces. Gently stir in walnuts and bean curd. Add sauce. Continue stirring quickly over heat until liquid is thickened. Serve immediately.

> 1 serving equals: 2 lean meat exchanges
> 1 bread exchange
> 4 fat exchanges
> 125 mg. sodium
> 303 calories

Vegetables

Almond Noodles (Makes 6 servings)

> **3 qts. boiling water**
> **1 tsp. vegetable oil**
> **8 oz. egg noodles**
> **1/4 cup slivered almonds**

1. Add vegetable oil to the boiling water.
2. Add noodles and bring to a boil again. Reduce heat to low (so water does not foam over) and boil, stirring occasionally, just until noodles are tender, about 7 minutes.
3. When noodles are tender, drain immediately and toss with almonds.

> 1 serving equals: 2 bread exchanges
> 1 fat exchange
> 2 mg. sodium
> 181 calories

Curried Corn-on-the-Cob (Makes 4 servings)

> **4 small ears of corn**
> **Water**
> **4 tsp. butter or margarine, unsalted, melted**
> **Dash of curry powder**

1. Remove husks and silky threads from the corn.
2. Cook 15 minutes in boiling water.
3. Add curry to melted butter or margarine.
4. Remove corn from water and place on platter for serving.
5. Dribble melted curry butter over the corn cobs, and serve.

> 1 serving equals: 1 bread exchange
> 1 fat exchange
> Sodium negligible
> 113 calories

Vegetable Medley (Makes 6 servings)

> **1/2 cup chicken broth, unsalted**
> **2 tsp. milder soy sauce (Kikkoman)**
> **3 Tbsp. vegetable oil**
> **1 cup cabbage, cubed**
> **2 carrots, cut in small strips and steamed about 3 minutes**
> **1-1/2 cups bamboo shoots, raw, cut into 1-inch lengths**

1 cucumber, peeled, seeded and cut into strips
1 cup snow pea pods
Freshly ground pepper to taste

1. Combine broth and soy sauce; set aside.
2. Heat oil in wok or skillet over medium heat. Add cabbage and cook, stirring constantly, about 3 minutes.
3. Add remaining ingredients; cook and stir 2 minutes longer.
4. Add broth mixture and cook, covered, 3 minutes over medium heat. Add pepper, and serve.

1 serving equals: 1 vegetable exchange
1 fat exchange
77 mg. sodium
70 calories

Salads and Dressings

Avocado, Cream Cheese and Walnut Salad (Makes 6 servings)

2 whole avocados
1 lemon
3 oz. cream cheese
2 Tbsp. walnuts, chopped
Lettuce leaves

1. Peel avocado, remove pit, and cut each fruit lengthwise into 3 wedges.
2. Squeeze juice of lemon over the fruit.
3. Mash cream cheese with a fork and place 1 Tbsp. in the middle of each wedge of fruit.
4. Sprinkle chopped walnuts on each wedge.
5. Place on lettuce leaves and serve.

1 serving equals: 1 vegetable exchange
3 fat exchanges
37 mg. sodium
160 calories

Basic Salad Dressing (Makes 1-½ cups)

1/4 cup red wine vinegar
1/4 tsp. garlic powder
1/4 tsp. dry mustard
Artificial sweetener to equal 1/2 tsp. sugar
1/4 cup water

1/4 tsp. fresh ground black pepper
2 Tbsp. lemon juice
1 cup vegetable oil

1.   Combine vinegar, garlic powder, mustard and artificial sweetener, and stir until dry ingredients are thoroughly dissolved.
2.   Add water, pepper and lemon juice; mix well.
3.   Stir in oil slowly. Pour into a jar with a tight fitting lid and shake vigorously for 2 minutes.
4.   Store, covered, in refrigerator.

1 Tbsp. equals: 2 fat exchanges
Sodium negligible
90 calories

Desserts

Fruit Dessert (Makes 4 servings)

2 small oranges, peeled and diced
1/2 small banana, sliced
10 dates, diced
1/4 cup coconut, shredded
1 Tbsp. sesame seeds
Dash Angostura Bitters

Combine all ingredients, toss gently, and serve.

1 serving equals: 2 fruit exchanges
1/2 fat exchange
3 mg. sodium
110 calories

References

1. *"Nutrition and the M. D.,"* Vol. IV, No. 5, page 1, March, 1978.
2. Kinsell, L. W., Stone, D. B., Behrman, D. M., Flinn, L. B., Hamwi, G. J., Pollack, H., Vester, J. W., and White, P. "Principles of nutrition for the patient with diabetes mellitus." *Diabetes 16*, 738, (1967). Bierman, E. L., Albrink, M. J., Arky, R. A., Conner, W. E., Dayton, S., Spritz, N., and Steinberg, D. "Principles of nutrition and dietary recommendations for patients with diabetes mellitus." *Diabetes 20*, 633, (1971). Wood, R. C., and Bierman, E. L., "New Concepts in diabetic dietetics." *Nutrition Today*, May/June, (1972), page 4. Lenner, R. A. "Dietary aspects of diabetes mellitus (abstract)." The VIIth International Congress of Dietetics, Sydney, May 4–10, 1977, page 110.
3. Stone, D. B., "A rational approach to diet and diabetes." *Journal of the American Dietetic Association 46*, 30, (1965).
4. Haunz, E. A., "Diabetes mellitus in adults." *Current Therapy* 1973. Silver Anniversary edition. Editor: Conn, H. F., W. B. Saunders Co., Philadelphia, (1973), page 365.
5. Tjokroprawiro et al., "Moderately high carbohydrate in diabetic dietetics." Diabetic Clinic of the Department of Internal Medicine; Airlangga University School of Medicine, Surabaya-Indonesia. Presented at VIIth International Congress of Dietetics, Sydney, May 4–10, 1977, page 16.
6. Brother, M. J., *Diabetes the New Approach.* Grosset & Dunlap, New York, (1976), page 103.
7. Travis, L. B., "An instructional aid on juvenile diabetes mellitus." University of Texas Medical Branch, Galveston, (1969), page 81.
8. Harris, R. S., Wang, F. K. C., Wu, Ying, H., Tsao, Chi-Hsuen S., and Loe, L. Y. S., "The composition of Chinese foods." *Journal of American Dietetic Association*, 1949, 25: 28–38.
9. American Diabetes Association, Inc. The American Dietetic Association, 1979, Exchange List for Meal Planning.
10. "Composition of foods, raw-processed-prepared," *Agriculture Handbook* No. 8, Agricultural Research Service, U. S. Department of Agriculture; 1963.
11. Food Composition Table for Use in East Asia; U. S. Dept. of HEW; December, 1972; by Woot-Tsuen Wu Leung, Ph. D.; Ritva Rauanheimo Butrum, M. S., and Flora Huang Chang, B. S., Federation of American Societies for Experimental Biology.
12. Bowes and Church *Food Values of Portions Commonly Used*: 12th Edition; J. B. Lippincott Company, Philadelphia; 1968.
13. "Nutritive values of some Hawaii foods in household units and common measures." Carey D. Miller and Barbara Branthoover; Hawaii Agricultural Experiment Station; Circular 52; June, 1957, University of Hawaii.
14. "Japanese-American food equivalents for Exchange List," *Journal of American Dietetic Association* Vol. 62., February, 1973; Perspectives in Practice.

156

15. "Chinese Diabetic Exchange List," North East Medical Services, San Francisco, Ca., February, 1972.
16. "Japanese Diabetic Exchange List," Toranomon Hospital, Tokyo, Japan 1965.
17. "Composition of Hawaii fruits," Hawaii Agricultural Experiment Station; University of Hawaii; bulletin No. 135, December, 1965.
18. "Nutritive value of American foods in common units," *Agriculture Handbook* No. 456, Catherine F. Adams; Agricultural Research Service, United States Department of Agriculture, November, 1975.
19. *Diabetes and Chinese Foods*, The Canadian Diabetic Association, January, 1978, Toronto, Ontario.
20. "Low sodium spice tips," American Spice Trade Association, Englewood Cliffs, N. J.
21. "Seasoning with spices and herbs," United States Department of Agriculture, Science and Education Administration, Consumer and Food Economics Institute, December, 1978.
22. "Sodium restricted diet," American Heart Association, New York.
23. "Sodium-restricted diet; The rationale, complications, and practical aspects of their use," National Academy of Sciences—National Research Council, Publication 325, July, 1954; Washington, D. C.
24. "Sodium in Chinese vegetables," Shirley Lew Chan and Barbara M. Kennedy, Ph. D., Department of Nutrition and Home Economics, University of California, Berkeley, July, 1960.
25. *Wok Talk*, The Chinese Grocer, San Francisco, California, 1980.

Index

158